The Best Beginner's Guide to Dogs and Puppies for Kids

The Best Beginner's Guide to Dogs and Puppies for Kids

Everything You Need to Know about Breeds, Training, Safety, and More!

Lynn Guelzow

Sky Pony Press
New York

Sky Pony Press books may be purchased in bulk at special discounts for sales promotion, corporate gifts, fund-raising, or educational purposes. Special editions can also be created to specifications. For details, contact the Special Sales Department, Sky Pony Press, 307 West 36th Street, 11th Floor, New York, NY 10018 or info@skyhorsepublishing.com.

Visit our website at www.skyponypress.com.

10 9 8 7 6 5 4 3 2 1

Manufactured in China, August 2025

This product conforms to CPSIA 2008

Library of Congress Cataloging-in-Publication Data is available on file.

Cover design by Kai Texel

Cover images by Getty Images

Interior image credits: Shutterstock unless otherwise noted. Getty Images, page 40, 129; Lynn Guelzow, page 18, 43, 99; Robert Guelzow, page viii; Matthew Peters, page 39; Rachel Primmer, page 48; US Customs Service, page 126.

Print ISBN: 978-1-5107-7203-8
Ebook ISBN: 978-1-5107-7290-8

To my lifetime of best friends, muddy paws, and cold noses: Freckles, Annie, Asta, Sarge, Rascal, Libby, Mickey, Atticus, and Jet; and to Sean, Madeleine, and Teagan, who were raised in a pack without complaint; and finally to Seth, who put up with fur in his coffee and made it all possible.

CONTENTS

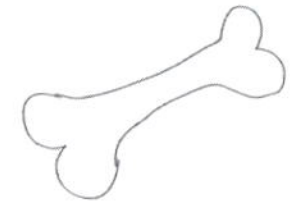

The author, at age eleven, hard at work at her neighbor's kennel.

AUTHOR'S NOTE

Two houses down from mine on our rural, country road, an older couple ran a small family business grooming, training, boarding, and breeding dogs. Their own kids were adults when I took my nine-year-old self down the road to beg them for a job. I was desperate to do anything that involved dogs. The roar of the barking at feeding time was music to my ears, although I suspect I was the only one in my family that found it enjoyable.

The couple, Bev and Roger Randrup, took pity on an eager kid who offered to work, and that was my introduction into the incredible world of dogs. I continued to work for them until I left for college. They introduced me to 4-H, where I trained and showed my first dogs. I adopted a Brittany Spaniel puppy from them and named her Annie. They allowed me to borrow their dogs—a gorgeous Afghan Hound named Olivia, and a Toy Poodle named Sadie—to experience a variety of breeds, differences in behavior, and training abilities.

Since then, I've added many dogs to my life, each unique in its own way. Some I went looking for, and some found me when I didn't know I needed them. Every dog taught me something, and I discovered the power of a strong relationship to overcome difficulties and problems. Dogs have trained me as much as I trained them. I'm excited for you to start this journey, too. Love your dog, build a strong bond, learn her needs, discover his quirks. You are in for an incredible experience.

1

A Short History of Dogs

Wolves

Thousands of years before there were dogs, there were wolves. It's believed that a small group of wolves lost their natural fear of humans and learned to live with humans as partners. This process is called *domestication*. Exactly how the wolf was domesticated is debated among researchers and scientists. Did humans tame wolves? Or did the wolves tame themselves? One theory is that wolves scavenged for food near human campsites and followed people as they traveled, gradually coming to depend on them. However it happened, over thousands of years, these domesticated wolves evolved into a new species: the dogs we know today.

SIMILARITIES BETWEEN WOLVES AND DOGS

- Keen sense of smell
- Sociable and prefer to live in a pack or family
- Same number of chromosomes
- Same number of teeth (forty-two)
- Both will "pant" to cool off
- Both raise their hackles and bare their teeth to show aggression

DIFFERENCES BETWEEN WOLVES AND DOGS

- Wolves avoid humans
- Dogs seek human companionship
- Wolves have much larger teeth
- Dogs have a smaller skull
- Wolves are heavier and taller than most dogs
- Wolves cannot be domesticated
- Dogs can be highly variable in size, coat type, and ear style.
- Wolves are more uniformly large and shaggy with pointed upright ears.

The fossil record shows a clear progression from the larger skulls and bones of a wolf to lighter bones and smaller skulls. Wolves and dogs are each other's closest cousins in the animal world. They share 98.5 percent of their DNA. But the Frisbee-catching, ball-retrieving dog we invite into our homes is definitely not a wolf in dog's clothing. A wolf, no matter how young it is and how you might try to raise it, would not behave like a dog. A wolf is a much more independent animal and can weigh as much as a human adult. And while a German Shepherd may look more like a wolf than a Toy Poodle, it's actually more closely related to the Poodle.

Wolves began roaming the earth about one million years ago, during a time called the

Pleistocene era. They were formidable hunters at the top of the food chain. Gray wolves, the largest in the canine family, can be up to six feet (2 meters) long and weigh as much as 170 pounds (77 kg). Wolves hunting in packs were able to kill very large prey such as woolly mammoth, caribou, horses, and sheep.

As humans came into contact with wolves, stories and myths were created with wolves cast as the antagonist. Many fables still told today feature wolves as scary predators to be feared. Stories such as "Little Red Riding Hood" and "The Three Little Pigs" depict wolves as fearsome enemies that would eat the heroes if not destroyed. A happy ending is a dead wolf in these old myths and fables.

More than two thousand years ago, the Scottish King Dorvadilla gave an ox as a reward to anyone who killed a wolf. Wolves were hunted ruthlessly for centuries. By 1680, there were none left in Scotland, but it wasn't the only place where wolves were systematically hunted. At their peak, wild wolves are estimated to have numbered in the millions but are now reduced to fewer than 300,000 worldwide.

Who Domesticated Who?

The fear that early humans had toward the wolf made it unlikely that wolves were brought in to settlements and towns and turned into pets. A newer theory is that the wolf domesticated itself. Perhaps less-aggressive wolves found benefits to living near humans and eating their leftover food. These less-aggressive wolves may have slowly adapted to life with humans by becoming smaller, friendlier, and more helpful. Any aggressive wolf would have been driven away or killed by the humans, leaving only the friendliest to continue interbreeding and evolving. These early wolf-dogs would have benefited from consistent food, the warmth of fires, and protection from other creatures. Humans would have valued the friendlier wolf-dogs as partners in hunting and alarm systems for intruders.

However the process of domestication happened, the first dogs appeared about twenty to forty thousand years ago. They may have been domesticated in one location and then spread out with humans, or there may have been multiple places where humans and wolves partnered up and created "the dog."

Scientists are using DNA analysis of bones and fossils to answer the question of when and where dogs were first domesticated. The earliest known

ALL IN THE FAMILY

Dogs are most closely related to the gray wolf. But there are several other members of the Canidae family. Scientists divide up animals that are similar into categories. Dogs belong to the Canidae family, which is a subset of carnivores, which is a smaller set of all mammals. All canids share similar characteristics that make them more closely related to each other than other carnivores (such as lions or bears). Wolves and dogs are the most closely related of the canids, but other members of the family include fox, coyote, jackal, dingo, and raccoon dog. Canids can be found on every continent except Antarctica. Of the entire family, none make good pets or have been successfully domesticated other than the dog.

Raccoon dogs live in east Asia, but came to Europe as part of the fur trade and exotic pet industry. Raccoon dogs can do a great deal of damage to local habitats where they have no natural enemies.

The Australian dingo is the largest carnivore in Australia and probably descends from domesticated dogs that were brought to the island continent over four thousand years ago and then escaped.

Jackals live in Africa and come in many varieties. They may hunt for food or scavenge what is left behind by bigger carnivores. They mate for life and live in pairs rather than in a pack.

DOGS THAT ARE NOT DOGS

Hyenas are not part of our dogs' extended family. Hyenas are more closely related to cats than they are dogs. The prairie dog is also not part of the dog family. Despite their name, a prairie dog is a rodent, not a type of dog.

dogs probably lived in China and Europe but could have developed in other parts of the world as well. By about 8,000 years ago, humans and dogs had formed a strong bond and were spreading out, together, across the globe. Archaeologists commonly find bones of dogs alongside those of humans throughout the world. Drawings of dogs in caves with humans are common. In France, the Chauvet Cave holds the imprints of a child walking alongside a large wolf or doglike animal. These footprints were left in soft clay about 26,000 years ago and remain, now hard as rock. They are some of the oldest evidence ever found of dogs and humans living together. Ancient cave drawings of dogs found in France are estimated to be between 12,000 and 15,000 years old. Saudi Arabia also has ancient cave drawings depicting dogs that are at least 7,000 years old. Cultures from Europe, Asia, North America, and the Middle East have ancient cave drawings or pottery showing dogs to be closely connected to the humans they lived with.

Dogs were the first animal to be domesticated and live in partnership with humans.

After dogs, humans began domesticating other animals and plants, and this began a fundamental transformation of human society. Humans gradually gave up hunting and gathering and turned to farming. Dogs were an important part of this process. Without dogs, farming may not

THE AFRICAN WILD DOG

Not all dogs are domesticated. The African wild dog is best recognized by its mottled coat and very large, rounded ears. It's also called the "painted wolf" or "painted hunting dog." These dogs live in sub-Saharan African and are endangered. They live and hunt in packs of about six to fifteen members, although a century ago packs could be as large as five hundred dogs and their population numbered in the hundreds of thousands. Currently their populations have dropped to about 1 percent of their former size. Human encroachment on the African wild dog's territory, reduction of the food that the wild dog lives on (gazelles and wildebeest) and hunting of the wild dog by farmers are the reasons for the dramatic decline and endangerment of this unique and interesting dog species. African wild dogs are descended from wolves and share some traits similar to our domesticated dog, but are a separate species.

GREYHOUNDS IN ANCIENT EGYPT

Dogs similar to Greyhounds were worshipped during the reign of the pharaohs of ancient Egypt. Many of the pharaohs were buried with their dogs in massive tombs. The Dog Star is part of the Canis Major constellation (also known as the Great Dog). When the Dog Star goes behind the sun, we call this the "dog days" of summer. Greyhounds were so revered during the time of ancient Egypt that when one died, family members would shave their heads and not eat while they mourned their dog.

have been possible. Dogs assisted humans in protecting other animals, such as sheep, goats, and pigs. A dog was an excellent guard and could hear or see approaching danger long before people did. A good dog would bark to alert people of approaching danger (perhaps a wolf, lion, or another human), defend the flocks, and help move flocks from one place to another.

In addition to protecting and herding goats and sheep, dogs proved to be very useful in everyday life to early humans. This is a short list of things dogs may have done to help their early human families:

- Protect homes and settlements
- Herd sheep, goats, and pigs
- Pull sleds and carry heavy loads
- Hunt deer, elk, wild boar, and other game

- Provide companionship
- Clean up food scraps
- Reduce rodents and other pests (a mouse makes a good snack!)

Dogs continue to do these same services today. Providing companionship has risen on the list and become the only thing many dogs do for most people. While much has changed, the close relationship between dogs and people remains. Our dogs feel like full family members in most homes, and some have taken on new and interesting jobs (*see also* chapter 10, Dogs with Jobs).

THE AMAZING AZTEC XOLOITZCUINTLI

The Xoloitzcuintli (or "Xolo" for short) is an ancient breed going back about 3,500 years in what is now Mexico. This dog was considered sacred by the ancient Aztec, Maya, and other Indigenous people. The Xolo was believed to have magical powers to ward off evil spirits.

Human history is full of the many contributions that dogs have made. Humans have honored dogs from the beginning of recorded time in temples, art, stories, and religion. As human cultures intermixed, our dogs adapted to our changing lives but remained our most trusted companions.

When ancient Roman seamen arrived in the islands off the coast of Africa thousands of years ago, they found the local people loved and honored dogs so much that the Romans named the islands the Islands of Dogs or "the ones with dogs." The Romans spoke Latin and the word for dogs in Latin is "canaria," which is how the islands got the name Canary Islands. The name stuck and later, when a small bird was discovered on the islands, it was named for the island. Most people believe that the Canary Islands were named for the bird, but it's actually the other way around. The Canary Islands continue to this day to have two dogs on their coat of arms and national flag.

WELCOME

2

Welcome Waggin'—Getting Your Home Ready

Maya and Ryder

Maya and her family were at a local fair when Maya saw a box of puppies by a farm stand. There was a sign on the box that the puppies were for sale. They were very cute and friendly, so she convinced her parents to buy one. She promised to take care of him and named him Ryder. They stopped on the way home to buy some puppy food at the grocery store. It was a Sunday evening and they all played with Ryder until bedtime. The puppy was exhausted and slept all night with Maya. The next day, Monday, they took the puppy outside, where he peed and pooped before the entire family left for school and work. They left the puppy loose in the house because he'd been so good the night before. When they came home the kitchen trash can was on its side and garbage lay all over the floor. Ryder had peed and pooped on the rugs. There were chewed pillows (feathers everywhere!) and newspapers and magazines had been shredded. It took hours to get the house cleaned up. The next day, they left Ryder in the backyard where he couldn't destroy the house. But when they got home, he'd dug holes and escaped under the fence. Luckily, a neighbor caught him and brought him back. Maya thought maybe this puppy was just bad, but the neighbor explained Ryder was being a normal puppy. Maya and her family agreed that they needed to learn how to keep Ryder, and their house, safe.

Successful Starts

Every puppy or dog needs a good, welcoming home. But it takes a little bit of planning before your new dog arrives. The most important thing is that you are willing to take on this responsibility of care. If you know what to expect, and your whole family is excited for a new dog, you are bound to be successful!

Before you go looking for a dog, you should spend some time thinking about what kind of a dog is going to be best suited to live with you and your family. Here are several very important questions you should ask:

- Where do I live?
- Where will I walk and exercise my dog?
- How young are the kids in my family?
- Do I have other pets?
- Is there anybody home during the day?
- Is this the first dog that my family has ever owned?

The answers to these questions will help you understand what kind of a dog is going to be best for you. Let's look at how the answers will guide you in your decision.

Where You Live

If you live in a city or an apartment, a large dog may not be a good idea. The large breeds (over fifty pounds, or 23 kg) need room and space to run and exercise. Young dogs have naturally boisterous natures and may be too much for an apartment in a city. Small to medium dogs are a good fit in small living spaces. Small dogs also need exercise and can develop a bad habit of barking when home alone. Most dogs can adapt to apartment living and do well if you pay attention to their exercise needs. They'll need to be taken for long walks outdoors. Dogs older than two years do not require as much play and exercise as young adult dogs and puppies. And as you'll see in chapter 5, some dog breeds need more exercise than others. Every home is different, but you can find a good fit if you plan before you buy or adopt a new dog.

Even if you have a yard, you may still need to walk your dog. A large dog in a small yard will find it difficult to get enough exercise. Bored dogs with lots of energy and not enough exercise can create big problems. If your yard is small, but you are planning to get a large dog, you should plan and prepare for daily leash walks to keep your dog happy. A small yard will be enough for your pup to relieve himself and stretch his legs, but he will need more leash walking every day to keep him fit and happy.

WHITE HOUSE DOGS

Almost all US presidents have brought one or more dogs into the White House to live with them during their presidency. Our first president, George Washington, was an absolute dog lover. He had many dogs and he gave them funny names, such as Sweet Lips and Mopsey. He kept Foxhounds, Greyhounds, Dalmatians, and many other breeds during his life. Washington's dogs probably lived at his home in Mount Vernon, Virginia, as the White House wasn't built until after he had left the presidency. Other presidents kept their dogs at the White House and some became quite famous.

Franklin D. Roosevelt, the thirty-second US president from 1933 to 1945, had a Scottish terrier named Fala. In 1940, Fala came to live in the White House with the president. Fala became quite popular and famous as he went with Roosevelt on many trips. Fala was dearly loved by President Roosevelt. Every day a bone was included on his breakfast tray for Fala while they lived in the White House.

Fala has his own statue in Washington, D.C., sitting alongside his famous owner.

John F. Kennedy, the thirty-fifth US president from 1961 to 1963, brought his family dog, a Welsh Terrier named Charlie, to the White House in 1961. Charlie was joined by a small white puppy named Pushinka (which means "fluffy" in Russian). Pushinka was a gift from the Soviet Premier Nikita Khrushchev. Pushinka was a mixed-breed dog that was notable for being the daughter of Strelka, the first dog sent to space by the Soviet Union. Pushinka had a litter of puppies in the White House. When they were old enough to be weaned, two were kept by Kennedy family members and two were given to winners of an essay contest created by First Lady Jacqueline Kennedy. The winners of the pups were two kids, aged nine and ten, from Missouri and Illinois.

Warren G. Harding, the thirty-ninth US president from 1921 to 1923, brought his Airedale Terrier to the White House. Laddie Boy was the first truly famous White House dog. Laddie Boy attended all cabinet meetings and had his own chair at the table. Laddie Boy was so popular that there were almost daily articles about him in the newspapers.

Age of Family Members

Very young children under five years old can be challenging for some types of dogs. If you have a baby or toddler brother or sister, a mellow breed like a Labrador, Golden Retriever, Poodle, or German Shepherd are typically more tolerant of small children. All of these breeds are known for their affection for and protectiveness of small children and family members. Babies and toddlers need to be protected. But it's also important that babies and toddlers not be allowed to pull the ears and tails of dogs or cause them pain. Closely watching very young children will always be necessary until the children learn that they should not hurt or crowd your dog.

Other Pets in Your Home

Birds, cats, gerbils, rabbits, reptiles, and even other dogs make wonderful pets, but they may not appreciate a new dog or puppy coming into their home. It is good to ask questions about a dog you may want to adopt to make sure they are okay with other pets. A dog that has chased or threatened cats will probably not be cured

of this if you have a cat in your home already. Dog breeds that are in the Hound Group (*see* chapter 5) will not be a good choice if you have birds or bunnies in your home. The hunting "prey" drive is a strong instinct, and these dogs may never understand that your pet bird is not something he can hunt.

Home Alone

A new dog should not be left home alone every day while the family is at work or school. Long hours alone can be a recipe for trouble. One solution may be to use a dog walking service or doggy day care to keep your dog happy and reduce his free time to chew on the furniture. These services can get expensive. Before getting a dog, your family should discuss whether you can budget for a dog walker. Another solution may be to get an older dog, one who is more than five years old and will be happy to sleep during the day while you are gone. If you really want a younger dog or puppy, but she will be left home all day alone, you will need to arrange for daily exercise and care.

First Dog

The first dog a family adopts is incredibly exciting. If you have no experience with a dog or a puppy, consider getting a young adult rather than a puppy. Puppies are teething and chewing machines that can destroy pillows and shoes in a matter of minutes. They also need a great deal of time spent potty training, teaching basic obedience, and playing to use up all the energy a puppy has. A young adult that is already house-trained and through the worst of chewing may be the best choice for your first dog.

When looking for that first dog or puppy, consider how much the breed sheds and how much grooming may be required. Breeds such as setters, collies, huskies, and smaller dogs with long silky hair require daily brushing and maintenance to keep their coats tangle free and clean. Dogs with a thick coat will shed enormous quantities of hair and need regular brushing to rid them of dead hair. Dogs with long droopy ears or skin folds will need regular care to keep them healthy. For a family's very first dog, a low-maintenance, short-haired dog may be the best option.

Prepare Before Your Dog Arrives

Before your new dog puts her first paw in the house, you can prepare to make her happy and welcome. Dogs don't need a lot of things, but there are a few essentials to get ready.

Dishes for Food and Water

It's best if food and water dishes are kept separate. Dogs are messy eaters and will drop food into the water dish if they are close to each other. To lessen your own cleanup and need to dump and clean the water, keep these two bowls apart and not on the same stand.

Tall dogs should have a food dish that is elevated. If your new dog is tall, such as a Great Dane, Irish Wolfhound, or other tall breed, set the food dish a few inches off the ground to make eating and swallowing easier.

Slow feeding dishes are a great solution to a dog that eats too fast (this is called "bolting" their food). Eating very fast can cause stomachaches or throwing up. A food dish that has a maze in the bottom will slow down your fast eater to a healthy pace.

Dog Bed

A bed for your dog to lay on can save your couches from fur and claw damage. Dogs prefer a bed that is cozy and allows them to curl up. Too small or too big will not be comforting. Try to find a bed that fits your dog. Use washable bedding until your new dog is settled and you are sure he won't chew the bed or use it as a toilet.

Leash and Collar

Your new dog will need a collar that fits properly. Get a collar that buckles or snaps on. Washable collars are good choices as they get dirty and smelly. Most are adjustable and can be expanded if your new dog is still growing. Add a name tag with your dog's name and your phone number in case she gets loose or escapes your yard. Do not use a slip collar (or choke chain) as these can get caught on objects in your house or yard and become very dangerous. Get a six-foot leash with a loop on one end. Six feet is the perfect length for walking and training. (More on training your puppy in chapter 7.)

Crate

You will need a crate that your dog can stand in and turn around. Crates are perfect for house-training and preventing her from chewing the furniture or shoes when you aren't home. The crate should be large enough for your puppy to grow into. If she is a young puppy who is expected to be very large when full grown, get a crate with a divider that you can remove as she grows.

Baby Gates

For the first few weeks, at least, confine your new dog to a single room, like the kitchen or family room. If your house doesn't have doors between the rooms, a baby gate (or two) is essential while your new dog is learning the rules.

Grooming Tools

All dogs need regular grooming. A soft brush for short fur, comb for long hair, and a nail trimmer are the essential tools. Don't forget gentle dog or puppy shampoo. Human shampoos often come with fragrance and are not good for a dog's skin.

Chew Toys

Two or three chew toys of varying shapes and bumpiness are great. Don't get too many chew toys or your dog won't know what a chew toy is and what it is not. Everything will seem like a chew toy. Dogs have preferences on what they like. Some really like rope toys, others prefer balls, stuffed squeaky toys, or hard bumpy bones. Whatever you choose, make sure at least one is hard. Hard chew toys will scrape her teeth and stimulate the gums.

Dog Food

Most dogs will do very well on a simple kibble diet. Most of the commercial foods are balanced to give your new dog all the nutrition, vitamins, and minerals that he needs. If you know what your dog was fed before coming to your home, keep him eating the same type of food for a few days until he's settled. If you don't know (many rescue dogs or shelter dogs come with little information), pick a good-quality food, or ask your veterinarian for a recommendation. Avoid wet or canned food.

Training Treats

You can buy training treats that come in small packages that are easy to handle and store. You can also use any food that is irresistible to your dog, such as chopped-up hot dogs or small bits of cooked chicken or liver. You will want to start reinforcing good behavior on day one. A tasty treat and praise every time she pees outside will make house-training a breeze. (See more on house-training in chapter 7.)

THE FIRST DAY AND NIGHT

From the minute your dog enters his new home, you and he will be building your relationship. It is easy to start building the positive, forever bond you both want and that humans and dogs have enjoyed for thousands of years.

Your relationship starts as soon as you pick up your new puppy. Touch her, play with her, and spend some time talking to her and petting her before you put her in the car. Cars can be stressful, so take your time touching and playing with her before you head for home. Let her smell you and lick you if she wants.

At home, let her walk around on a loose leash outside. Let her sniff and relieve herself after the drive. Don't go straight into your home if she hasn't had the chance to pee.

Once inside, keep her in one room. Let her sniff and explore. If she circles and sniffs, take her outside right away as that is a sign that she is about to pee.

Keep her company and watch her carefully. Sit on the floor and play with her. Take her outside frequently.

Let your puppy or dog meet all the family members at her own pace. Don't force her to be picked up or petted if she's scared or anxious. Give her time to greet all the kids and adults in the family. Ask young children to sit on the floor and let your new dog or puppy come to them.

Where will the new puppy sleep? There is no right or wrong answer. If she is a puppy and not yet

house-trained, keep her in the crate overnight while you sleep. The crate can be in your bedroom, the kitchen or den, or anywhere that you have decided is the room where you want the dog to sleep. She will need to sleep in the crate at night until she is completely house-trained.

For older, potty-trained dogs, you can choose to let her sleep on a dog bed or with you. There is no right or wrong answer. It is up to you where your dog sleeps and whether you and your family are okay with her sleeping on a bed or other furniture.

Before you bring home your new puppy or dog, find out if she's had all necessary vaccines and is healthy. You may need to have a veterinarian give her a checkup. Trips to the veterinarian may be stressful. (See chapter 9 for more about keeping your puppy or dog healthy.)

Where Should You Get a New Dog or Puppy?

You want your new puppy or dog to live in a house with you. The best way to know your dog will be able to live happily in your home is if he is already happily living in a home. Puppies raised or fostered in a home have the best chance of easily moving into your home. Good breeders will raise just one litter at a time in their home. Rescue groups will foster puppies in volunteer homes. Both of these are great ways to know your new dog will have a good experience living in a home. You may be able to visit before making the decision.

Avoid buying a puppy or dog from a pet store. You will not have any way to know how the puppies were raised or socialized. All puppies are cute in a store and their friendly behavior is not a good way of knowing how they were handled and raised. Pet stores may purchase puppies from puppy mills. These are places that breed lots of litters of puppies all the time and do not care well for the parent dogs or the puppies.

Animal shelters have a wide variety of puppies and dogs. Shelters might be run by your city or town or by a private group. Shelters take in as many dogs as they can and provide an important way for dogs to have a second chance with a new family. You may not get very much information about your new dog from a shelter. Sometimes there is information about the dog's past, but sometimes there isn't much at all. Shelter dogs make excellent pets, and you might find your perfect furry friend in a shelter.

FOSTER HOMES NEEDED

Not quite ready to make a lifetime commitment to a dog? Many rescue organizations don't own a kennel or have a place to keep dogs while they are waiting for a new home, so they rely on people and families to volunteer as foster homes for dogs. A foster family may have an adult dog for just a few days or weeks, sometimes longer, before a lasting, "forever" home is found. Foster families usually pay for food, but veterinary costs are paid for by the rescue group. It's a great way for new dog owners to see what owning a dog is like, knowing that you won't have him for very long. If you already own a dog, fostering can give your dog a new friend to play with.

There are lots of reasons to become a foster family, but the main one is that you will help a dog make the transition from one home to another. Dogs that end up in rescues will have some stress. Change is upsetting for dogs and people. Foster families make that change easier for dogs in need. As a family gets to know a dog in their home, they will be able to help decide what kind of new home would be best. For some foster families, the dog they care for turns out to be a perfect fit and they decide to keep him or her. Fostering is a great way to help dogs in need.

3

Puppy Power

Diego and Ruby

When thirteen-year-old Diego and his family brought Ruby, a Golden Retriever puppy, into their home, Diego was thrilled. Ruby was twelve weeks old when she came to live with them, and she had lots of energy and loved to play. Diego walked her every morning before school and they developed a little game. When Ruby saw him getting his shoes on for her walk, she would spin in circles, bark, and grab his shoes. As Diego tied his shoes, Ruby would pull the laces and untie them. Diego tried to race her to see if he could tie his shoes before Ruby untied them. His dad warned him that teaching her to bite his shoes was not a good idea. Diego thought the game was harmless, and she didn't bite hard enough to hurt him. But one day, Diego came home from school and couldn't find his soccer cleats. He looked everywhere—under his bed and in his closet. After much searching, Diego found the cleats in the backyard. Ruby was happily chewing on the laces, while his ruined shoes lay in tatters next to her.

Early Life of a Puppy

A puppy is any dog less than one year old. During the first year of life, puppies will do most of their growing, learning, and mental development. Large-breed puppies, such as Great Dane or Saint Bernard, seem to grow right in front of you as you watch them, and even smaller breeds will grow very quickly the first six months of life. Small- to medium-sized dogs will reach full height around eight months of age, with larger breeds growing for almost two years. The growth is just as fast inside a puppy as outside. Their brains and bodies are going through enormous changes. At two months, you can run faster than most puppies, but at three months, it's a race. At four months, the puppy will almost always win.

Before puppies leave their mother, they learn many things from each other and from Mom. A group of puppies born together is called a *litter*, and each puppy in the litter is a *littermate*. A litter can be as small as one puppy or as big as fifteen, but most litters are between four and eight puppies.

Born Blind, Deaf, and Toothless

Puppies are born with their eyes tightly closed. They are toothless and their ears are sealed shut. They are guided by smell and touch in those first few days. Their mother and littermates are their whole world. Puppies are vulnerable and need the security of a safe nest and a protective mother. After about two weeks, their eyes begin to open but they still can't see well. When they first open, a puppy's eyes will be blue, but they will slowly darken to a brown or amber color. In a small number of breeds, such as the Siberian Husky, one or both of their eyes may remain blue for their entire life. After eighteen days of life (or about three weeks), a puppy's ears will begin to unseal. It takes about a week for their ears to completely unseal and their hearing to improve. Once their ears are fully open and developed, puppies will hear far better than humans. A puppy can hear sounds from four times farther away than humans can. They are able to hear at far greater frequencies and ranges. A puppy will hear notes that are both much higher and much lower than what you are able to hear.

THE FIRST TWO MONTHS

During the first two months of their life, puppies rely on their mother for cleaning, feeding, and care. As they grow, they begin to play and compete for food. Puppies learn how to control their bodies, they gain strength and speed, and they learn not to bite hard or risk a strong reaction from a littermate or their mother.

- From birth to ten days, puppies have little interaction with the world. Born with eyes closed, they cannot see or hear and have little awareness beyond their most basic needs of hunger and warmth. They will double their birth weight in the first seven to eight days.
- By two weeks of life, puppies are beginning to see and hear. They learn that the other soft blobs around them are other puppies. Their world view is limited to their mother and their littermates.
- At three to four weeks, a young pup is learning to move and walk on her own. Her stomach will drag on the ground. She stays with her mother in the nest and will not venture out on her own. A three-week-old puppy may be able to crawl away a few feet, but her mother will gently carry her back into the nest.

- Human contact and interaction should begin after three weeks. Puppies should learn to trust and accept human touch, petting, and being moved or picked up and spoken to. Puppies have little immunity to diseases and should not interact with other animals or people other than the person caring for them and their mother.
- Puppies can begin to eat soft puppy food at three weeks and will no longer need to nurse from their mother after four weeks. This process of switching from their mother's milk to solid food is called *weaning*.
- At eight to nine weeks, puppies are ready to leave their mothers and littermates to go live with their new families. This is the youngest age for a puppy to be bought or adopted.
- At eight to nine weeks (two months of age), pups are clumsy but can now walk and move about on their own. This is a good time to introduce a variety of smooth and rough surfaces, like wood, grass, or cement, to build tolerance and acceptance. As they learn to clamber over different types of surfaces, they will gain confidence and will be able to handle slippery or hard pavement with ease when they are older.
- At about eight weeks, puppies begin to show fear of strangers and new situations. This is normal. Don't react to their fear with big displays of comfort, soothing, or petting. Instead, let the puppy investigate at their own pace. If you remain calm and confident, your puppy will learn not to fear people or new situations either. Continue to introduce your puppy to a mixture of people (old and young, male and female) over time. His fear reaction will subside, and he will learn to trust the people you bring into his world.

The Importance of Play

During these early months, puppies are learning through play all day long. Experts believe that puppies use play for many reasons—to gain strength, to practice skills such as stalking prey, and to learn how to get along in a pack. These lessons are essential to normal development. Most of the things you teach a puppy will involve play. Rolling a ball for a young puppy and encouraging him to chase it and bring it back to you can be an important foundation for later skills. While most dogs will learn to chase a ball with little effort, getting them to bring it back and give it to you is harder. Use a tasty treat to reward them when they bring the ball back to you and drop it. Start early in simple ways, rewarding with treats and praise, and he will learn important lessons, such as coming when called and giving you objects. This is a first step to teach obedience in a fun way. As your puppy gets older, you will be able to teach him to catch a Frisbee or run farther to catch balls.

Socialization

Puppies need positive human contact starting at two to three months of age. Introducing a puppy to people, other pets (like cats or birds), and all the things they may encounter in the world is called *socialization*. Socialization is very important for a puppy. A puppy must learn that the world is a safe place and that her new family will love her and protect her. It's important to give your puppy many experiences to socialize her. She should ride in the car and visit stores, parks, and other areas where people and dogs may meet. When guests come to visit, a new puppy should learn to accept your friends without barking or jumping on them. (See chapter 6 for tips on how to train a puppy to greet people politely.) As she learns that guests in the house are not a threat, she will look forward to these visits and act calmly. These activities will help her grow into a good family member.

Puppyhood lasts until about one year of age. Small dogs will reach adulthood earlier than large dogs. During the first six months of life, a puppy will grow very fast. A puppy needs extra nutrition during this time. Puppy kibble is a good choice to meet your puppy's needs. The hard crunch of kibble will help a teething puppy's gums and new teeth feel better. A good-quality food made just for puppies is a great choice. Table scraps are not a good diet for a growing puppy because leftover human food is not nutritionally balanced. Some human foods that are very safe for us can be dangerous to a puppy or dog.

All puppies and dogs need to learn how to behave. Teaching them in a positive, rewarding way is faster and more effective than scolding or punishing them. Even when we

DANGEROUS FOODS FOR DOGS

- Chocolate
- Coconut
- Grapes and raisins
- Macadamia nuts
- Onions

DANGEROUS PLANTS FOR DOGS

- Aloe vera
- Azalea
- Begonia
- Castor bean
- Sago palm
- Leaves and stems of tomato plants

CRATE TRAINING

A crate is a useful tool that can help a puppy adjust to life away from her mother. It should never be a punishment. Dogs instinctively prefer a small, comfortable den that gives them protection from other animals. A crate should be set up like a "den" for a puppy. It should be big enough for her to stand up and move around inside without bumping into the sides. A crate should include soft bedding for comfort and a cover for privacy and a sense of security.

A very large crate will feel too spacious and not provide the close comfort that a den would. If the crate is too large, the puppy may have toilet accidents in it, feeling that the corners are far enough away from the den. Crates will keep a puppy safe from getting into hazardous items. A puppy should not roam a house freely without being watched until teething is complete, and she no longer has accidents in the house.

A crate is an excellent tool for house-training and preventing destructive chewing, but a puppy will not be happy if left in a crate for many hours at a time. If no one is home during the day, have a friend or dog walker stop over several times to give her potty breaks, exercise, and socialization.

get angry if a puppy damages something, yelling or hitting is never a good idea. Chapter 6 will help you teach good manners in a positive way.

The first year of a puppy's life is an important time. A tremendous amount of growing and learning happens. Owning a puppy is very rewarding, but there's a lot of responsibility as well. Puppies need consistent interaction and attention. An adult dog may tolerate being left home better than a young puppy. Early manners can be taught as a part of play. As your puppy runs toward you, reinforce this behavior by saying her name, praising her and repeating the "come" command. Always use praise to let her know when she is doing well.

Puppies are certain to make many mistakes as they grow. Owners of a young puppy need to have patience and time. If all the members of a family are at school or work most days, a puppy may not be a good choice for your family. A young pup will need to learn to relieve himself outside, but he won't be able to hold his bladder for more than an hour or two when he's very young. The more frequently you can take your pup outside to relieve himself, the faster and easier the house-training process will be. See chapter 7 for more on how to house-train your new puppy.

TEETHING

Puppy teeth emerge around three weeks of age. Puppies usually have twenty-eight small, sharp teeth. Around three to four months (twelve to sixteen weeks), these puppy teeth fall out. Puppies often swallow these teeth while they are chewing or eating, but it's possible you could find them around the house. They look like translucent grains of rice. New, adult teeth slowly come in and by the time the puppy is six months old, all the puppy teeth are gone and the puppy will have forty-two permanent adult teeth. During this time, the puppy will need to chew. Some puppies prefer knobby toys. Almost all puppies like to chew on hard objects like bones. Give your puppy appropriate teething toys to chew on. If your puppy chews on things he shouldn't, quietly take away the object and redirect him to a toy that he should chew on. Never spank or hit your puppy for chewing. Chewing is an important and normal activity for a puppy. Your job is to make sure he's chewing on puppy toys and not your shoes, houseplants, or furniture.

Puppies and dogs are very social animals and do not do well if they are isolated. Puppies that are left alone all day will be unhappy and may develop anxieties and problem behaviors that can last their lifetime. A puppy will have trouble sleeping at night when the rest of the family goes to bed if the puppy has slept all day. How much time a puppy will spend alone should be talked about before a puppy is brought into the home.

If your family decides that raising a puppy is the right choice, you are in for a rewarding and *fun* experience! Puppies love to play and will provide you constant entertainment and affection. Watching her grow and teaching her all the things she will need to know as an adult will build a strong family bond between the people, puppy, and other pets you might have.

After Diego's shoes were destroyed by Ruby, he didn't let her play with his laces. The next time he tied his shoes, he told Ruby, firmly but gently, "No!" when she tried to grab the lace. Diego immediately gave Ruby her favorite rope toy to chew on instead and then praised her when she took the toy instead. After several days of Diego consistently reinforcing the message by handing Ruby the toy when she went for his laces, she stopped pulling on shoelaces and instead went and grabbed her toy herself!

All puppies can learn to be good family members. No puppy wants to misbehave. If we learn what our puppies need, we can help them grow up to become awesome adults. Read on to learn all about awesome adults in chapter 4.

4

Adults Are Awesome

Devon and Toffee

Devon dreamed of getting a puppy he could raise right from the start before anyone taught him bad habits. Devon was sure a puppy would be perfect. His parents felt that it wouldn't be fair to a puppy. Devon's baby sister was just one year old, and his parents were busy with work and taking care of his sister. They thought an older dog would work better for their family. Devon agreed to go look at the dogs in the local shelter, but he was sure he wouldn't find any older dogs he liked. All the dogs looked happy, but none were as cute or cuddly as a puppy. One of the last dogs they saw was a Wheaten Terrier about two years old. He'd been given to the shelter when his previous owners moved into a home that didn't allow dogs. His name was Toffee, and he was house-trained and well-behaved. When Devon called to Toffee, the dog tilted his head on the side, seemed to consider

Devon, and walked over to him. Toffee leaned against Devon's leg and wagged his tail. Devon was in love. Toffee knew how to fetch and had lots of energy but was much easier than a puppy. He didn't need as much training and could be trusted to sleep with Devon right away. Devon realized that Toffee was a great dog that just needed a good, safe family to love him.

Adults Make Excellent Pets

Sometimes people wrongly think that if an adult dog is in a shelter or a rescue, then there must be something wrong with it. Sometimes there may be a behavior problem, but more often, dogs just need to find a new family due to a problem that has nothing to do with them. Great dogs might be given up because their family is moving to a place that does not permit dogs, a human family member may have an allergy to the dog, or the family does not have the time or ability to care for the dog. Older dogs may have developed problems or bad habits in prior homes, but often, they are not serious. "Problem" dogs are usually dogs that were never trained. These dogs will make excellent pets for a new family that will teach basic manners. Puppies may be cute, but adult dogs are awesome. Consider an adult dog, over one year of age, if you are getting a new dog.

Adult dogs will have outgrown many of the worst puppy behaviors by age one. An adult dog will have all of her permanent teeth and be past the teething stage. An adult dog will be more settled and less excitable than a puppy, will sleep through the night better, and will be more capable of being left at home while kids are at school and adults at work.

PERSONALITY TESTING

Every dog has his own unique personality. Some dogs are braver, some are shyer, some are quick to bark, others are very chill and unbothered by new things. How your dog behaves and reacts is part of his *temperament*, or his personality. If you want to know more about your dog's personality, the American Temperament Testing Society has a test you can do with your dog. Dogs must be at least eighteen months, or one and a half years, old to take the test. Any breed or mixed breed can be tested. The test is to see how your dog will react to strangers, loud noises, and unfamiliar situations. The last phase of the test is an angry, scary stranger. Some dogs panic and try to run away, others might try to attack. Most dogs become alert and watchful, which is the safest for all. The stranger does not hurt the dog or come very close.

Doing a temperament test can be interesting and you will learn a lot about how your dog's brain thinks and reacts.

Your adult dog will need exercise to keep his weight at a good, healthy level. Play is a great way to keep him fit and continue to build your relationship together. Playing tug-of-war with a rope toy is one of the easiest games you can play with your dog. If you don't have a lot of space to throw a ball, tug-of-war may be better.

Another excellent way of keeping your adult dog fit is to walk or jog with him on a leash. Taking your dog for a walk is some of the best exercise for a dog, and he will really enjoy it. As dogs get older, they may want to play less. Dogs enjoy walking with us, and they like to jog, if that's more your speed. A daily walk in the morning and the evening may be all the exercise your adult dog needs on a regular basis. As long as your dog stays fit, he

surprise from the dog

don't leave it

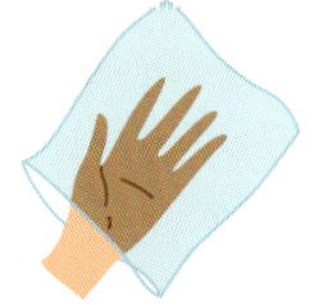

put the bag on your hand

pick up dog surprise

almost done

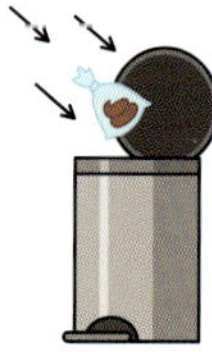

throw in the trash

HOW TO CLEAN UP AFTER YOUR DOG

will be able to enjoy longer, more intense activities on weekends or vacations.

Whether you are at a dog park or walking your dog somewhere else, picking up your dog's poop is an essential part of being a good owner. Cleaning up after your dog is not just good manners, it will also reduce the spread of disease.

Getting Older

The saddest part of dog ownership is knowing that they age faster and die sooner than the people who love them. A dog may be fully mature by one year of age and elderly at twelve. Few dogs live past the age of fifteen. As our dogs get older, they need special care. Your black lab may be able to jog five miles with you at age six but unable to do more than walk around the block at age eleven. Older dogs have all the same issues that older people do, they just happen faster to a dog. Older dogs get arthritic, sleep more, and become less and less active. They may develop tooth issues and need softer food that is easier to chew. Their eyesight might get worse. Many older dogs get cataracts, just like older people do, making it hard for them to see.

Despite these issues, many older dogs try very hard to continue doing everything without slowing down. These dogs need their owners to take it easy and reduce stress and strain on their bodies for them. If your older dog vigorously chases a ball one day and then limps and can barely get up the next, he probably overdid it. Play for short periods of time and have her do less running and jumping. If she is hurting after play, rub her

DOG PARKS AND SOCIALIZATION

Dog parks are common in many cities and towns. A dog park is a great way to get exercise and social interaction for your dog. Adult dogs do best at a dog park as puppies can be overwhelmed by the other large adult dogs running around. For dogs and owners who don't have a fenced backyard, a dog park is a great way to let your dog burn off extra energy and safely play with other off-leash dogs. You should only bring

your dog to an off-leash dog park if he's friendly with other dogs and people. While treats are an important part of most training, don't bring any food (including training treats) into the dog park. Other dogs will know you have food (their noses are very good, even if you have it in your pocket or a cooler). Other dogs may not have good manners, especially around food. To be safe and reduce the risk of dog fights or aggression, leave the food and treats in the car or at home. Check out any rules at your local dog park before you go, but here are some common things you should always do when at a dog park:

- Don't go if your dog isn't vaccinated. You don't want to spread or catch any diseases.
- Pick up any poop your dog makes.
- Leave any food at home or in the car.
- Keep your leash with you at all times.
- Keep your dog's collar (with an ID tag) on him at all times. If he should escape through a gate, it will help to catch and return him to you.
- Collars should be buckle or snap, with no chains or dangling collars that can get tangled or choke your dog when playing with others.

Most importantly, if your dog shows aggression to other dogs or may start a fight, don't take him to the dog park. This is not the place to work through aggression problems. Fights between dogs in a dog park are scary and can cause serious injury to dogs and the people trying to stop the fight.

muscles and ask your vet if there is a mild pain reliever that will help keep her comfortable and active.

Dogs age at different rates. Small dogs tend to live longer and large dogs live shorter lives. Very large breeds like Great Danes and Mastiffs might live six to ten years. A little dog, like a Yorkshire Terrier or Toy Poodle, may live as long as fifteen years or more. Dogs of different breeds or mixed breeds may age at very different rates. Here are some signs that your dog is getting older:

- Cloudy eyes and losing sight
- Difficulty getting up or moving more slowly
- Stinky breath
- Sudden change in weight
- Peeing accidents, especially while sleeping
- Hairs on the muzzle turn gray

Your older dog will enjoy attention and grooming but will also sleep more and need shorter walks and playing sessions. Talk to your vet about normal aging for your type of dog. Our older dogs can enjoy a good quality of life if we are patient and make changes for their comfort. More gentle petting and less play can keep your older dog happy and content.

VACATIONING WITH YOUR DOG

When the family goes on vacation, what should you do with your dog? Gone are the days when the only option was to take your dog to a kennel. Now, many hotels and other vacation rentals will happily allow you to bring your pet with you. You can search for hotels that allow dogs and plan your trip so the entire family can stay together. There are a few things to plan and pack to make sure all goes well.

- Extra leash and collar
- Poop pickup bags
- His usual kibble or food needs for the entire trip
- Packable, collapsible water and food dishes
- Copies of his current veterinary paperwork showing vaccinations or health certificate

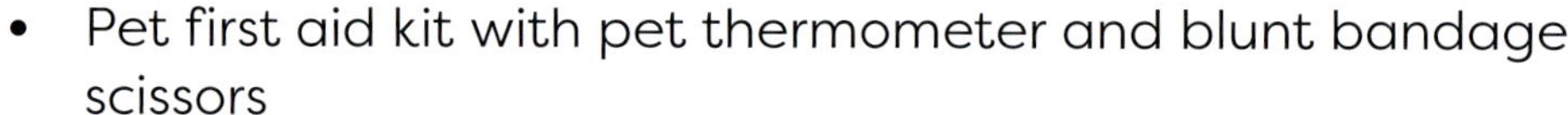

- Pet first aid kit with pet thermometer and blunt bandage scissors
- A favorite blanket or chew toys to keep him entertained while confined
- A pet carrier for your car or a seat belt harness to keep him secure while driving

Dogs enjoy vacations as much as we do. Many cities allow pets to travel on public transportation. Campgrounds, national and state parks, beaches, and hiking adventures are all great vacations to bring your dog along. A well-mannered dog that does not bark and disturb other guests, and owners that clean up after their dog, are welcome in many popular vacation places. Resources are available on the internet to help you plan a trip that includes the four-legged family members on your trips.

If you cannot bring your dog along, make sure that he is well cared for at home while you are gone. Most dogs would prefer to stay at home rather than go to a kennel or boarding facility. A good pet sitter will keep your dog comfortable while you are away. Make sure they can come over several times a day to relieve your dog and are willing to spend some time playing with him and making sure he's getting exercise and social interaction.

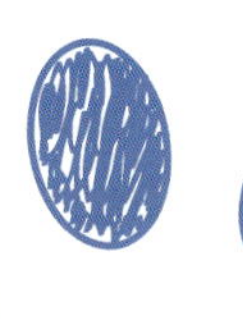

5

Mutts, Purebreds, and Everything In Between

Aditi, Spark, and Jasmine

Aditi's family has had two dogs for as long as she can remember, Spark and Jasmine. Spark is a white-and-brown spotted dog they adopted from a shelter when he was a little puppy. Jasmine is a purebred beagle that they purchased from a breeder when she was a small puppy, too. Aditi and her brother took both dogs to obedience class, but Spark was much better at it than Jasmine. Jasmine had no interest in learning to heel, sit, or stay, although she was willing to do things for a treat. At night, when the two dogs were in the backyard, Spark would chase a ball and play with Aditi, but Jasmine only wanted to sniff, dig, and howl. Aditi was convinced that Jasmine was dumb, and Spark was smart. On the other hand, Jasmine was super sweet, she loved to snuggle, and nothing bothered her. Loud noises like thunder and visitors never upset her. Spark hated thunder and many other things frightened him too. He would shake or whimper when scared.

Aditi asked the obedience trainer why the dogs were so different when they were raised together from early puppyhood in the same house. He explained how breed differences and instincts can be just as powerful as training and care. Jasmine and Spark were both smart, but in very different ways. Their big differences in looks and behavior were due to differences in breeding.

Small Started It All

The human-dog relationship was defined by the jobs a dog could do for thousands of years. The better a dog was at a job, the more valuable it was. Humans learned that if you had two large brown dogs and they had puppies, you'd get more large brown dogs. If you had a dog that excelled at finding and chasing down antelope, that dog would be enormously helpful. Humans realized that parent dogs passed along physical traits, like size and color, and mental traits, like guarding or hunting. Large dogs that could hunt and guard served everyone's needs. So how did we get small ancient dogs? What purpose would they serve?

SURGERY FOR APPEARANCE

You may see a dog with no tail or ears that point upward in an odd way. There are a few breeds that have a tradition of changing a dog's appearance using surgery. All dogs and all dog breeds are born with a long tail. If a tail is missing, it is probably because someone cut it off, likely when it was a newborn puppy, for fashion. Ears may also be trimmed and forced to stand upright. An example of this is the Doberman Pinscher. The Doberman is a breed developed in Germany around 1890. It is sleek, noble, and intelligent. Tails and ears are surgically altered. Doberman puppies are born with floppy ears and a long tail.

The surgical changes do not help the dog. Natural ears and tails do not need to be changed, and surgery provides no benefit to the dog. These are cosmetic things done for the preference of owners. European countries have banned ear cropping, but it is allowed in the United States.

It is hard to shrink down a big dog to lapdog size. The careful breeding it took to make a small dog made the whole process long. Many generations of breeding only small dogs to small dogs would get the resulting lapdog. Only rich people had the ability to spend that much time breeding tiny dogs for the fun of it. Think of them as the diamond rings of dogs. A small dog that served as a companion was a luxury only the rich, or the regal, could afford. Small dogs might be given as a gift between kingdoms. The desire for a valuable small dog led humans to understand a great deal about how to select parents to shrink the size of puppies and the dogs they grew up to be. There were no specific breeds at first. That all came later.

Ancient humans preferred small dogs for companions and to show that they were rich and privileged. Less-wealthy humans needed good hunting dogs and good guard dogs. People created different kinds of dogs to do many different kinds of tasks.

Dog Groups

We now classify dog types into seven major groups. These groups are kept track of by the largest canine organization in the United States: the American Kennel Club (called the "AKC" for short). The seven groups of dog breeds, according to the AKC, are the following:

- Herding group
- Hound group
- Sporting group
- Terrier group
- Toy group
- Working group
- Non-sporting group

Herding Group

The herding group has all the breeds that love to work with sheep or cattle (and even reindeer!). These dogs are some of the smartest in the dog world and the easiest to train. Breeds in the herding group include all of the collies and shepherds, such as Border Collie, German Shepherd, and Old English Sheepdog. The herding breeds form very tight bonds with their human families, much like the bonds that shepherds and their dogs have had for thousands of years. The intelligence of these dogs makes them suitable for many things other than herding sheep around. The one thing they aren't good at is doing nothing. These dogs will give themselves jobs if none is provided to them. They can be highly destructive and excellent escape artists.

WHY DO DACHSHUNDS LOOK SO FUNNY?

The Dachshund is a small German breed that was originally used to hunt and kill badgers. Dachshund actually means "badger dog" in German. Badgers are mean, furry carnivores that burrow underground. Fighting a badger head-on underground in a tunnel requires a fair bit of courage and independence. Battles between badgers and Dachshunds could go on for hours.

The body of a Dachshund is tunnel shaped and extra-long to provide protection from a badger's claws. Its legs are short to improve its ability to dig and squeeze through a tunnel. A dachshund's narrow face with long nose keeps its eyes away from the badger and gives the dog plenty of teeth to fight. Dachshunds rarely take on badgers anymore, but their exaggerated shape had an important purpose. These lapdogs can be ferocious and will not back down if threatened by a much larger animal.

Hound Group

The hound group contains dogs like the Basset Hound, Bloodhound, and Dachshund. Hounds are good hunting dogs, but they search for mammals, not birds. They are bred to find rabbits, antelope, or other animals that run on foot rather than fly. Some breeds rely more on their noses to track game ("scent hounds") and some rely more on their eyes ("sight hounds"). Bloodhounds are famous for their amazing ability to track scents over long distances and time. Sight hounds, such as the Greyhound and Saluki, combine speed with excellent vision. Hounds can make great family dogs, but be prepared for their instinct to follow their noses and eyes wherever they take them.

Sporting Group

The sporting group has some of the most popular dog breeds in it, including the Cocker Spaniel, Irish Setter, Golden

Retriever, and many others. Dogs in the sporting group love to hunt and chase birds. They also are good swimmers and have plenty of athletic abilities to wander fields, swim through ponds, and hike difficult trails. For an active family that likes to be outdoors, a sporting group dog could be a great fit.

Terrier Group

The terrier group are excellent at tunneling underground in search of rodents. These smaller dogs were bred to dig and find small creatures. Popular terrier group breeds are the Parson Russell Terrier, Scottish Terrier, and Bedlington Terrier. These dogs are best described as feisty and energetic. They have strong personalities and a tough, stubborn streak. You should also be prepared for a dog that really, really likes to dig.

Toy Group

The toy group are the smallest dogs bred to be lapdogs and

companions. They come in many colors, with short or long hair and big personalities. Toy breeds are known to be very social and can easily adapt to different lifestyles. Breeds within the toy group are the Chihuahua (from Mexico), Toy Poodle (from France), and Shih Tzu (from China). Tiny dogs are popular the world over. Don't let their small size fool

GIANT DOGS

The giants of the dog world are remarkable for their size and good nature. Truly big dogs come with their own big challenges. Without trying, their noses will be right at table and counter height. They can cost more to keep, eat more, need larger beds, and require larger supplies and equipment. Not all vet clinics will be able to treat very large dogs. X-ray machines, exam tables and other equipment typically found at a neighborhood vet's office may be too small for the biggest breeds of dog. Before bringing a very large dog into your family, check with your local vet to make sure they can handle and treat your big guy. Even with the best of care, the biggest dogs have the shortest lives.

Giant dogs, despite these challenges, are gentle and protective of their human families.

- Great Dane
- Irish Wolfhound
- Mastiffs (Bullmastiff, Neapolitan, and Tibetan)
- Scottish Deerhound

you, these "toy breeds" are not toys. They are smart, energetic, and sometimes sassy.

Working Group

The working group has big dogs that were bred to do hard or brave things, like the Great Dane, Saint Bernard, and Mastiff. These huge dogs pulled sleds or wagons, guarded homes, or rescued lost hikers and skiers. Dogs in the working group are big, rugged, and strong. Those from the mountain regions are well-insulated with thick, warm coats.

Non-sporting Group

The non-sporting group is a hodgepodge of dogs that don't fit into any other group. This group has the biggest variety of size, color, and purpose. The only similarity they all have is four feet and a wet nose. This group includes the American Eskimo Dog, Bulldog, Chinese Shar-Pei, and the Xoloitzcuintli.

Mixed Breed or Purebred?

A purebred dog means that all of its parents, grandparents, and other ancestors were all of the same breed. If you also have a certificate from the American Kennel Club for your dog or puppy, it is a *registered purebred*. Whether you have a dog that is purebred or mixed breed (parents and grandparents are not of the same breed) is a personal preference. Both mixed-breed and purebred dogs make great pets.

FLUFFIEST DOGS

Dog fur comes in many different colors, lengths, thickness, and texture variations. The fluffiest of dogs needed thick fur for insulation in the coldest of climates. It is not surprising to find so many of the fluffiest dogs originated in mountains or very cold countries. The thick fur of these dogs keeps them warm no matter the temperature. They may have double layers that seem to stand straight up. In the spring, they will "blow" their coat and shed out massive amounts of fur. Then they grow it all back in the fall. These dogs will fill your house with fur year-round. Make sure you have plenty of grooming tools and don't mind finding fur everywhere in everything.

- Great Pyrenees
- Bernese Mountain Dog
- Samoyed
- Newfoundland
- Leonberger

If you adopt a purebred dog, you will have a good idea of how big she will get and what she will look like, how long her fur will grow, and what she may like to do or be good at. A female Golden Retriever puppy will grow up to be a medium to large dog (about sixty pounds for an adult) and have yellow (light blond to darker golden) fur. She will shed lots of hair and be friendly and trainable. She will be very interested in birds and may point at them with no training and love to swim.

For people that want to know what they are getting and have a strong preference, a purebred dog will be predictable. Mixed-breed and purebred dogs are all dogs; neither is better than the other.

Most mixed-breed dogs are accidental. No one planned the litter and didn't breed the parents on purpose. However, some mixed breeds are being created on purpose. Mixed breeds will have traits from all of the breeds that went into them, but it's hard to know which breeds the puppy will favor more than others.

The Poodle is frequently mixed with another breed to attempt to get the best of both parents. For example, a Labradoodle is a mix of Labrador Retriever and Poodle. A Cockapoo is a mix of Cocker Spaniel and Poodle.

Poodles do not shed and are highly intelligent and easy to train. Mixing a Poodle with a Lab creates a dog that may shed less or not at all and is very friendly, athletic, and intelligent. There's less of a guarantee with a mixed breed. You might get what you are hoping for, but you might not.

Dogs that have parents from many breeds are sometimes called "mutts." They may resemble one breed more than others, but it's impossible to tell what they may be by looking at them. Mutts are usually bred by accident, not on purpose. There is a myth that mutts and crossbred dogs are smarter or healthier than purebreds. This is hard to prove one way or the other. The care and socialization that a puppy is given early in life probably matters more to its long-term good health than whether he is purebred or not.

6 Manners Matter

Luna and Jaxon

When Luna and her family adopted Jaxon, a mixed dog of the Boxer and Labrador breeds, his energy and friendliness won their hearts. The foster family that cared for Jaxon recommended obedience training to help him learn good manners. For two weeks, Luna's family let Jaxon adjust to his new home, but his behavior was terrible. He jumped on guests, barked whenever someone came to the door, and almost pulled Luna's arm out of the socket when he chased after a bicycle on one of their walks. Luna agreed to take Jaxon to a training class near their home. After six weeks, Jaxon behaved much better. Luna enjoyed the training and kept going to classes and working with Jaxon at home. One afternoon, she took him for a walk off-leash on a path. He trotted quietly at her side for most of the walk, but near the end he lurched forward off the path. Luna saw a dark shape in the bushes and thought it looked like an opossum. Jaxon stood still, staring eye to eye with the animal. Luna called out sharply, "Leave it. Jaxon, Come!" The training worked. Jaxon turned and came to Luna without hesitation. She praised him and snapped the leash on. She breathed a sigh of relief at the close call as Jaxon could have hurt the animal or it could have scratched or bitten him if he'd chased it.

Why Manners Matter

Dogs with poor manners can be annoying, distracting, and inconvenient. Very poorly mannered dogs may also pose a danger to themselves and their family. A large dog that jumps up to greet guests can knock people over, hurting or bruising them, and frightening people that don't know the dog. Even a small dog can cause bruising if it jumps or nips at people. It can be aggravating to walk a dog of any size that pulls on the leash or lunges and barks at other people or dogs.

Good manners are more than a "nice thing to have" when it comes to canine family members. Good manners are essential for dogs in any family. While everyone hopes their new dog will come with good manners built in, the reality is that you will probably have to do some training. Dogs are excellent students, learning quickly what behaviors you want. Unfortunately, they can just as quickly learn what you will tolerate and what you will ignore. Dogs will happily train the people in their lives, so it's best to start with some consistent ground rules that both you and your new dog can live with.

Every Dog Can Learn

No matter your dog's age, she can learn good manners. The old saying, "You can't teach an old dog new tricks" is just not true. It may take more patience and time for some dogs, but good manners and simple obedience are achievable by all dogs. Obedience training works best for most dogs if you remember a few general rules:

1. **Keep sessions short and sweet.** Short, frequent training sessions are better than one long training session. Dogs, especially young dogs, have a short attention span. Working for an hour or more is exhausting for you and your dog. Plan to train for five to ten minutes, several times a day.
2. **Make training fun.** Use toys, treats, and praise to reward your dog when he gets it right. At the end of a training session, toss a stick or ball if your dog

enjoys it as a reward for a good effort. Some dogs respond better to a favorite squeaky toy than food. Use the reward that your dog values the most.

3. **Be consistent.** Always use the same commands for the same behavior every time. For example, the command "down" should always mean lying on the floor.

Don't say "down" when your dog jumps up. Using the word "down" for two different things (lying down and not jumping on you) is confusing to your dog. Another example is sometimes saying "come" and other times saying "come here" or "here, girl." Pick one word for the command and use it every time you want her to come to you.

4. **Equip yourself for success.** Use a six-foot (2-meter) leash and a well-fitting collar for most training. Long retractable leashes are not good tools for training, and your dog can slip out of a loose collar. If you have a puppy, get a collar or harness that can be adjusted easily as your puppy grows. Avoid training collars that cause pain or fear, such as electronic collars or collars with spikes.

5. **Mindset is important.** If your dog is high-energy, let her burn off some energy chasing a stick or playing in the

backyard before starting a training session. Once she has had a chance to use up some energy, it will be easier for her to pay attention and succeed at training.

6. **No force necessary.** Never hit your dog with your hand or an object. Pain and fear are not effective dog training methods.

Reward good behavior only. "You get what you pet" are true words you need to remember. If you pet your dog when he's acting badly, you will get more bad behavior. Never reward whining, barking, or other bad behaviors with petting or attention (even if you are just trying to calm your dog). Giving attention with petting or soothing will result in more of that kind of behavior.

The Five Things Every Dog Can Do

Every dog can learn at least five things. Teaching these five commands will help improve your dog's manners and are the building blocks for more advanced training. I will walk through teaching each of these

BREEDS AND BEHAVIOR

While all dogs can learn good behavior, some breeds are naturally better, and quicker, learners than others. Being smart is not always best, but these breeds are known to be the easiest to train and enjoy advanced obedience. These breeds have an excellent mix of intelligence, willingness to please, and a good work ethic.

- Border Collie
- German Shepherd
- Labrador Retriever
- Papillon
- Poodle
- Rottweiler
- Vizsla

five commands. Practice consistently every day until your dog responds correctly the first time you give a command.

1. Sit

Start kneeling or standing next to your dog (kneeling is easier if you have a small dog). Your dog should be standing on all four paws. With one hand hold a food treat above your dog's head and slowly bring it back over his head. Your dog should follow the treat up with his nose. As the treat moves up and over his head, his butt will naturally lower. If he sits, say the word "sit" as you let him have the treat. If he is not sitting, you can gently press

down with the hand that was holding the harness. As soon as his butt touches the floor, say "sit" and give the treat.

Don't make him hold the position. Praise and give a release word such as "OK" or "free." Repeat the exercise several times, each time wait to give the "sit" command until after he is sitting. You are teaching him the meaning of the word. Your dog has to understand what "sit" means before you can expect him to sit on command. After a day or two of practicing this, ask him to sit while he is standing, holding the treat in your hand, but not lifting it over his head. If he sits promptly, give the reward and praise him. If he doesn't, just go back to raising the treat over his head slowly as you did the first time.

Never repeat the command "sit" if your dog doesn't respond the first time. He's telling you that he hasn't learned the meaning of "sit" yet and needs more practice. After several days of practice, your dog will sit just by you saying "sit" without having to push his butt down or raise a treat slowly over his head. At this point, say his name (to get his attention) and then the command to sit. Praise and reward with treats for several more days until you are sure that he knows what "sit" means and responds every time by sitting.

You should show your family members how to ask your dog to sit so that everybody in the family asks the same way. Your dog should listen and respond to everyone in the house, so ask your family members to practice the same way you do.

2. Stay

A dog that will stay put when told to will be much safer in the world. Stay is incredibly useful when you want to answer the door without your dog running through it to greet guests or escape. Stay will help your dog develop patience and confidence. Your dog needs to know that if you leave her, you will return. Teaching stay builds this confidence and her trust in you. However, nervous dogs or dogs with a lot of anxiety and fear may take longer to learn "stay." You will have to be patient and build her trust that you will return.

To teach your dog to stay, first ask her to sit. She should sit the first time you ask without encouraging. If she doesn't, go back and teach sit until it is solid in her mind. Teaching stay is best done with a leash on so you can catch your dog quickly if she gets up or moves away from you.

- When she is sitting quietly with you standing next to her, raise your hand with a flat palm. Hold it in front of the dog and say her name and "stay."

- Keep your hand in place, keep looking at your dog, and move your leg that's farthest from your dog away one step, then bring your other leg away so you are now standing on both your feet one step away. Don't drop your hand.
- Step back next to your dog, praise her quietly, and give your release word (such as OK or free).
- If she stayed for your one step away and then returning to her side, keep practicing just the one step away and back.
- If your dog gets up or moves toward you before you give tell her "free," gently put her back to where she started and try again. Take a smaller step away until she understands not to move and that you will return to her side.

- As your dog gets confident about staying for one step, try two steps. Gradually increase the distance and time that you ask her to stay. Practice several times, but keep your training time short. The goal is for you to be able to walk to the end of the six-foot leash, pause for a few seconds, and return to her without her getting up or moving around.

Stay is hard, and she may not be able to stay for more than a few seconds at first. At the end of your training, get down on the floor with her for a longer cuddle or playtime. Make sure she knows you are happy with her effort. If she gets up or moves, don't get angry or frustrated. Learning to stay can be hard for some dogs. Go as slow as she needs. Every dog learns at her own pace. Believe in her and be patient and positive, and she will succeed.

3. Come When Called

Your dog needs to come no matter what else is happening in his world. Learning to come when called may save his life. It is the most important skill you may teach him. Even in the best yard and with the most careful attention to doors and gates, your dog may become loose. It happens. It's best to prepare for the possibility and teach him to return to you when called.

The best way to teach your dog to come is to have a friend or family member help you.

- Have your friend hold the leash while you walk a short distance away (about six to ten feet, or two to three meters).

- Sit down on the ground and hold your hands (with a treat) out so your dog can see you
- Look happy, welcoming, and friendly with a big smile
- Using a happy, high voice, call your dog's name and say "come" as soon as she starts to take a step toward you.
- Your friend can encourage her if she doesn't come by walking toward you and gently tugging on the leash.
- When your dog gets to you, greet her enthusiastically ("Good Girl!") and give her the treat.
- Most dogs will come readily to their owner if you are sitting down on the ground and have a treat.
- Practice coming a short distance with a friend several times, always praising and giving her a treat when she gets to you.

If you don't have a friend to help, put a long, light line on your dog's collar. Any long, lightweight rope or light leash will do. Let your dog wander around the yard on her own. When she gets a few feet away, do the same as above, sit or kneel on the ground and call her with a happy, cheerful voice. If she doesn't come right away, be patient and encourage with a gentle tug on the line. Stay happy and cheerful in your voice and welcoming in your body movements. Don't drag her in or try to reel her in like a fish. She needs to come on her own. Call her and tug once, be very cheerful, and make sure she knows you have a treat. Even if she's slow the first couple of times you try, give her a lot of pets and praise when she comes to you. With practice, she should come more quickly. Keep using treats until she is confidently coming as soon as you call her.

When you feel she is coming every time you call, it's time to reduce the number of treats. Give a food treat less often, but always praise her and be cheerful. Keeping a leash on while you are teaching your dog to come is very important. You will need to keep her from leaving until she understands what you want her to do.

Sometimes, we accidentally teach dogs to do the opposite of what we want. Coming when called is one of those things. You can train your dog *not* to come very easily and without meaning to. Here are two examples:

1. Your dog has gotten into the trash and made a mess while you were gone. You call your dog over to you to point out the mess and tell him "Bad Dog!" in an angry voice. If you are mad at your dog, don't call him and yell at him. He will think you are mad because he came when you called him.
2. You've taken your dog to the dog park and she's been playing happily with other dogs. She's having a great time running and chasing with other dogs. When you want to go home, you call her and put the leash on to leave. You have now taught her that when you call her, playtime is over. She will believe that coming when you call means no more playing.

Both of these examples show how you can teach something when you don't mean to. So, what should you do instead? In the

CLICKERS

Clicker training was first developed to train dolphins in the 1960s. It works using a distinctive sound (a click) followed by a food reward or praise to positively reinforce good behavior. Clickers are very inexpensive tools that can be purchased at pet supply shops or online. With training and practice, the "click" sound becomes associated with good behavior and positive feedback. Dogs trained with clickers become enthusiastic and willing learners. The click sound "marks" or indicates that the dog has done a good thing. Timing of the click is the most important part of clicker training. Using a clicker is different from praise or treats alone as it makes very clear to the dog that he has done something correctly. Dogs trained with clickers have been able to learn very complicated and demanding tasks. Clicker training can be fun for both human and dog with very good results. Dogs develop a "what are we learning today?" attitude and are excited when they see the clicker. Training can feel more like a game, and results can be impressive and quick.

first example, calm down and don't get angry. If your dog is engaging in destructive chewing (or going through the garbage) when left home, she may need to be crated or to stay in a dog pen, rather than left loose in the house. (See chapter 8 for more on dealing with destructive behavior.)

In the second example, the easiest way to solve the problem is to call your dog many times at the park, give her a treat and praise, and let her go back to playing. Don't call her only when it's time to go home. Call her, with a lot of praise and enthusiasm and treats, then let her return to play with the other dogs. At the end of the play session, make sure to praise her, pet her, and give her a reward for coming before you put the leash back on to go home.

4. Down

Down is the last of the basic commands. Now that you've mastered sit, stay, and come, it's time to teach him to lay down quietly on the floor when asked. Teaching down will come easier now that he knows the other basic commands.

- Start by kneeling or sitting on the floor near your dog. Make sure you have several treats.
- Ask your dog to sit.
- Hold a treat in your hand and lower your hand *slowly* to the floor near his front paws. Don't slide your hand away from your dog or he'll get up to follow the treat.
- As his nose follows the treat down, wait for him to lay down.

- When his elbows touch the ground, say his name and down: "Jack, down."
- Use a calm voice and let him have the treat
- Practice several times until he goes down quickly when he sees your hand lower to the ground.

Now you can practice all four commands when you are training. Repeat daily and ask him to sit or lay down randomly during the day. The more practice he gets of all four commands, the more he will understand each word means something in particular that he needs to do.

The more you praise him and offer treats for good efforts, the happier your dog will be to train with you.

5. Leave It

Teaching your dog to ignore things he really wants to investigate is potentially lifesaving. No matter how careful you are, your dog will likely find something dangerous, toxic, or disgusting that you do not want him to eat, play with, or roll on. Teaching him to "leave it" is critical. Even if you are standing right next to him, you'd be amazed at how fast he can swallow something. In order to avoid expensive trips to the veterinarian to have things removed from your dog's stomach, teach him to "leave it" on command. Here are the steps to teaching "leave it":

- Wearing shoes (not sandals) and standing next to your dog, show him a delicious treat. Say "leave it" and put it under your foot.
- If he tries to scratch, dig, or nibble at your foot, ignore him.
- As soon as he looks away or gives up, even for a second, tell him "good boy" and give him a treat (not the one under your foot).
- As long as he does not try to dig or scratch or bite your foot, keep rewarding him with treats and praise.
- Pick up the treat under your foot, show it to him, tell him to "leave it" and put it back under your foot.
- Give lots of treats as long as he continues to ignore it.
- Repeat this sequence several times until he looks away or backs away from your foot with the treat as soon as you

say "leave it." Give lots of rewards for ignoring the delicious thing under your foot.

- Within a few days, if he's understanding the command and ignoring the treat under your foot, try backing away a couple of inches. He should look away from the exposed treat, not grab it. If he grabs it, go back and practice the earlier steps until he does not try to grab the treat when you say "leave it."

Now that he understands the command, find lots of other ways to practice in the real world. When you walk past an object that is super attractive to him, say "leave it" cheerfully and stand still. The second he looks away from the object, praise him and give him a treat. He needs to ignore it without you tugging or restraining him. When he turns to you and ignores the object, praise and give treats.

"Leave it" will be useful for so many things. Once he knows leave it, you can safely walk him without fear he will drag you off in pursuit of a squirrel or the neighbor's cat.

7 House-Training

Giovanni and Tesora

Giovanni was a little angry. His three-month-old puppy, Tesora, had just peed, again, on the carpet in his bedroom. This was the third time in almost the same spot. His room was starting to smell bad. He mashed some paper towels down on the spot and threw them away, but he didn't know how to stop Tesora from messing in his room. He'd played with her in the backyard for a really long time, and she didn't pee there at all. He figured she didn't need to go. He went inside to get a snack and while he was in the kitchen, she'd gone upstairs and peed in his room. Giovanni did not understand what was going wrong and why Tesora couldn't figure out to pee outside, not in his bedroom.

What happened with Giovanni and Tesora shows several common mistakes that people make and how these mistakes lead to problems with house-training a new dog or puppy.

House-training can be done quickly and reliably. Every dog can learn to go to the bathroom outside. How long this takes and how successful you are depends on you, not the dog. If your dog is having bathroom mistakes in the house, don't blame your dog, blame yourself.

The Foolproof Method of House-Training a New Dog or Puppy

You will need a crate that fits your dog. This is critical, and there is no substitute for a good crate. A small room or closet will not result in foolproof house-training. You need a crate and there just is no better way.

Your puppy will spend a lot of time in the crate for the first week, so it should fit her well. She should be able to stand up and turn around without bumping her head or body. It is okay if her tail wags and hits the side of the crate. Either a hard-sided plastic crate or a wire crate are good. If you have a wire crate, you can cover the top with a blanket or slipcover that makes her feel less exposed and safer.

Your puppy will sleep in the crate at night with the door closed. In the morning, she will need to go to the bathroom. Take her outside as soon as she wakes up. Take her to the area you would like her to use for her bathroom needs and simply wait. Walk her quietly and give her plenty of opportunity to go. Don't play or try to get her to run around. You don't want her to be distracted. She may need to pee more than once. Give her time to finish all of her business. When she does go, praise, pet, and reward with bits of food treats especially if she is one of the breeds that is difficult to house-train. You can't praise her too much, so go ahead and make a big deal out of any successful peeing or pooping outside.

Make sure she knows just how happy you are

BREED DIFFERENCES

Believe it or not, some breeds of dogs are much easier to house-train and some are much harder. The "hard" dog breeds can learn and become fully house-trained, but it may take longer, with more accidents, and will require more patience from you. For the difficult breeds, it isn't a lack of "smarts" or intelligence. They may care less about being clean and may be more stubborn about doing what they want to do. These dogs are independent thinkers. Crate training and positive food rewards are the best tools for house-training these breeds. The "hard" breeds are also a little more difficult to obedience train. If you have a dog that is one of these breeds, or a mix of any of these, you may have to be very patient and consistent in your training to get a good result.

- Afghan Hound
- Beagle
- Bloodhound
- Dalmatian
- Mastiff
- Pekingese

that she did it correctly. After she pees, you can play if she wants to. She may want to explore and sniff the yard. You can continue to walk or play. Some dogs have a lot of energy first thing in the morning, and you can play as much as you want after she has done her toilet business.

When you go inside, she can have a few minutes of playing and freedom in a small room (probably your kitchen or living room) where she spends most of her time. Make sure she has a chance to drink water.

After a few minutes of indoor play, return her to the crate with a chew toy stuffed with kibble. This is a good way to feed her slowly and keep her busy and happy while in the crate.

Every hour, take her out of the crate and go directly outside to where you want her to pee and poop. Every time she successfully goes to the bathroom, give her lots of praise and a treat.

If she doesn't go to the bathroom outside, come in and return her directly to the crate. Wait about fifteen minutes and take her back out and try again.

Whenever you are inside, put her in the crate when you can't watch her closely.

Continue to do this all day, taking her out every hour until bedtime. Puppies older than four months may be able to stay in the crate for more than an hour and still be comfortable. Younger puppies need to go every hour.

By using this method, you are using her natural instincts to stay clean to help her learn where to go to the bathroom. Most dogs will need to go potty about five to ten minutes after eating and when they wake up from a nap. Watch for when she eats, drinks, or wakes up and take her out right away for the best success.

For the first day or two, she will spend a lot of time in the crate. Make sure she has one or two chew toys (stuffed with her kibble) to keep her happy. She will not need separate breakfast or dinner feedings; she can eat all the food she needs by stuffing it into chew toys. She will need to work hard at getting her kibble out to eat, and this will also keep her busy. She won't get bored if her tongue is busy getting kibble out of a chew toy.

PEEING WHEN STARTLED OR THREATENED

Timid dogs may pee a small amount during times of stress or excitement, such as when their family comes home, visitors arrive, or they feel threatened. This is a misunderstood behavior. People make the mistake of thinking the dog has had an accident or that house-training isn't working. Neither is true. The name for this behavior is *submissive urination*, or peeing when threatened or scared. Timid, shy dogs might pee if you raise your voice or when adults come home and use loud voices to talk. For a dog, slinking on the floor or peeing a little bit is a sign that she respects your authority and does not want you to hurt her.

To stop the behavior, build her confidence. Don't ever yell or scold her, which will only make the problem worse. Crouch down to her level when you greet her. Try scratching her chest gently rather than patting her head. Always use a soft, warm voice when speaking to her. Let her know you aren't trying to be the boss, which will only frighten her. Sitting on the floor, petting her gently, even letting her win in games of tug-of-war will help her be more confident and less likely to pee in fear.

House-Training If You Aren't Home All Day

Not everybody can take a puppy or young dog outside every hour. That is the best method, but if you just can't have a family member, friend, or neighbor take your puppy out frequently, you can try using an exercise pen to help you through the early days of house-training.

You should never leave your puppy in a crate for hours, as it's just not possible for them to "hold it" for several hours at a time when they are so young. Locked in a crate, he will be forced to pee or poop in the crate. This is a difficult mess to clean up, and it teaches the puppy the wrong thing. It will teach him to pee where he is, even if he doesn't like it. It will make your house-training harder.

THE DON'TS OF HOUSE-TRAINING

- Don't hit him with your hand, a newspaper, or anything else
- Don't let your puppy or young dog loose in the house unless you are watching him *closely*
- Don't play until after he goes potty outside
- Don't rub his nose in his own pee or poop

THE DOS OF HOUSE-TRAINING

- Do use treats to reward him every time he pees or poops outside
- Do tell him he's a "good boy" and praise him
- Do play inside *only* after he pees outside
- Do watch him every minute he is loose in the house
- Do clean any soiled carpet or floor with an odor killing cleaner
- Do use a crate when no one is watching your dog

Instead, get an exercise pen. Put his crate in one corner and leave the door of the crate open. Put newspaper or an absorbent "wee wee" pad on the other side of the exercise pen, as far from the crate as possible. Put chew toys filled with kibble and a water dish near the crate. Most dogs will pee on the pads. They have a scent that encourages dogs and puppies to pee on them. The pads will protect floors and teach your dog to "go" in the same place. As your puppy gets older, you will have to remove the pads and transition your puppy to peeing outside only. In the end, he can be reliably taught to always relieve himself outside, but it may take a bit longer.

House-Training Issues

Most issues come about because the dog is loose in the house and not being watched. Making sure you are using the crate and keeping a close eye on your dog will eliminate most problems.

If your puppy has accidents in the crate, it is likely that she's been left too long locked in the crate and just couldn't hold it. Try to take her out more frequently and see if that helps.

Another problem can happen if you believe she is trained and you stop using the crate too soon. If your fairly reliable dog is suddenly having accidents in the house again, start over and be patient, with lots of treats for success. The patience and effort will be worth it.

8

Common Problems and How to Deal with Them

Noah and Arlo

Noah loved Arlo, a two-year-old black Labrador mix his family adopted from a shelter a year ago. Arlo loved to run and play. He would chase tennis balls for hours. He learned quickly not to mess in the house or chew up the furniture, because they'd used a crate for the first month Arlo lived with Noah and his family. Arlo was mostly a good dog. His biggest problem was jumping on people when they came in the door. He was so big that he could knock people over. Noah's grandma did not like the jumping at all. She got hurt once when he jumped up and scratched her arm. Noah was worried about that. He wanted his grandma to visit but was afraid she'd get hurt by Arlo.

Noah's mother found a trainer that would come to the house to help solve this problem. The first question the trainer asked was what they each did when Arlo jumped up on them? Everybody had a different answer. Noah's father would say "no," very loud and push Arlo away. His mom would say "down," and back up so Arlo wouldn't land on her. Noah's little brother let Arlo jump up because he thought it was funny and he didn't care about being jumped on.

The trainer spent the first day talking to the whole family about how to react to Arlo and making sure everybody said the same thing and did the same thing when Arlo tried to jump up on them or their guests. It seemed to Noah that a dog trainer spends more time training people than dogs. The trainer laughed and said that was true. Most dog problems are actually people problems.

What Causes Problems?

Dogs can quickly develop problem behaviors that are confusing to us. It's hard to understand why your dog jumps on you when you tell him not to, digs huge holes in the backyard, begs for food and drools during dinner, or barks at every sound in the neighborhood. Even worse, some dogs show aggression, growling and snapping for no reason you can see. Biting can be the most serious problem and can cause terrible injuries. Most problem behaviors are best prevented and can be very hard to fix after the fact.

WARNING! WARNING!

Dogs can't speak our language, but they try to tell us how they are feeling in their own way. When a dog is feeling anxious, upset, or even angry, she will give warnings. If you ignore those warnings, she might lose her trust in you, shut down, and stop responding at all, or even bite if she feels she needs to protect herself. Learn to recognize the warning signs from dogs.

Fear

Her ears will be down or back. She may be shaking or trembling. Her lips are tight and the corners are pulled back. Her tail will be down or between her legs. You may see some white on the edges of her eyes. This is a dog that is afraid.

Anger or Aggression

An aggressive or angry dog will go very still and rigid. He may curl up his lips and show his teeth. He will growl very low or give a short low bark. He may "muzzle punch" and hit you hard with his nose. None of this is "play" behavior. A dog that shows any of these signs could be dangerous.

If you meet a dog that shows either fear or anger, you should leave it alone. Don't attempt to pet it or touch it. A fearful dog may bite if you try to approach her. For both dogs, you should step back slowly, keep your eyes down, don't look directly at the dog's eyes, and don't scream or yell. Try to stay calm and only speak in a low, quiet voice as you slowly back away. Giving the dog some space and showing you are not a threat is enough to avoid most bites.

The best way to prevent problems from happening is to be consistent in your behavior and never reward (even accidentally) bad behavior. Your dog is a pro at figuring out what will get him what he wants. For example, imagine your dog wants to go for a walk. He tries to get your attention by nudging you. Then he goes to get the leash and drags it around. Then he barks and jumps around. Finally, you become annoyed at the barking and distraction, so you put the leash on him and take him out to make him stop barking and running around. Once the leash is on, he becomes even more excited. He bumps into you, spins in circles, and barks even more. By the time you get the door open he's so happy and excited he can't wait and barges through, almost knocking you over.

If this is your reality, think about it from your dog's perspective. The way to get you to take him on a walk is to bark, circle, jump up and down, and act like a lunatic. Most bad behaviors are like the annoying dog demanding to go on a walk. Every time you snap a leash on to his collar after a loud, rambunctious display, you are rewarding him and teaching him that the way to go for a walk is to bark, jump, spin, and act horribly.

Your dog will do whatever behavior gets him a reward. If barking and spinning get him a walk, he will do more barking and spinning.

Here are quick tips for ending bad behavior and starting a new routine:

- Praise him and give him attention when he's sitting or laying quietly.

- Notice when he's being good and reward it.
- Ignore barking for your attention.
- Get out the leash only when he's quiet.
- If he starts spinning, barking, jumping, or other bad behavior, put the leash away and ignore him.
- Wait for him to sit before putting the leash on.
- Wait for him to sit before opening the door.

Breaking a bad habit will take time. Don't give in, even if the barking and poor behavior get much worse. He must learn that the only way to go for a walk is to settle down and be quiet. But just as important, you can't ignore him when he's being good. Bad habits can be broken but only if you notice and reward good behavior all the time.

Preventing bad behaviors from starting is best. If your dog has learned a bad behavior that you want to end, it can be done. Telling her to stop jumping, stop barking, or to "be quiet" won't work. You will have to be careful to notice and praise good behavior and never reward bad behavior with attention, a walk, play, or food.

Digging

Most dogs will dig if given the chance. Digging is a very normal behavior for dogs. If there are interesting things to be found under the ground, like moles, gophers, or chipmunks, your dog will find this almost irresistible. You can't stop a dog from wanting to dig, but you can limit when and where he digs. Prevention is the most important part of the process. If you don't want your dog to dig up the garden or the backyard, don't leave him loose to wander around and dig holes when you aren't there. Some dogs just really like to dig and there is almost no way to cure them of this. Terriers will dig any chance they get. If you have a terrier, she may even dig in a flowerpot if that's the only dirt she can find.

If your dog is obsessed with digging, you have some options.

- Create a spot where you teach your dog to dig that won't bother you or destroy the yard or garden.

- Make fencing "dig proof" by putting chicken wire along the bottom. This will prevent digging under the fence and escaping.
- Fence off the garden or flower beds so he can't get in. Soft garden soil is a favorite for digging dogs.
- Redirect his behavior by offering a chew toy, playing a game of fetch or tug, or taking him on a walk.

STEALING FOOD

Dogs can smell delicious food. They know when something wonderful is on the table or counter. Some dogs will even jump up on the table or counter and take the food.

Teach your dog to always sit before feeding her. Don't feed her from the table, only put food in her dish. Feeding her table scraps is fine, but don't give her food from the table. Put it in her dish every time you feed her. She needs to know that the only food she can eat is what is in her dish. If she has already developed the bad habit of stealing food, you will have to keep food out of reach or watch her closely when food is out. When she is never successful at stealing food from the table or counter, she will stop trying. Don't create this bad habit by feeding her off the counter or table.

Fence or Leash Aggression

A dog that runs along a fence line barking and snarling at anything on the other side is dangerous. Another form of this behavior is a dog that lunges or barks aggressively at people or dogs when on a walk or on a leash. Both of these problems stem from the same cause—the dog is worried that there could be a threat and he is unable to respond because of the fence or leash. This is called *restraint frustration*. The dog is frustrated by the fence or leash and acts with anger and aggression. Very often, dogs that bark aggressively at another dog on a leash are more than happy to play with them when off the leash.

Not only is it scary, but it's very hard to stop once a dog has created the habit of barking at things on the other side of the fence or while on a leash. It is much easier to prevent than it is to stop. The best way to prevent fence running and barking is to make sure your dog is not left alone in the yard and allowed to run up and down the length of the fence. He will just get more excited and frustrated. A solid fence that he can't see through is one solution. Often a dog has no problem with fences if he can't see things on the other side. When you are with your dog in the yard, reward him for coming and playing with you. Don't let him get focused on the fence and what is on the other side. The more you keep him away from the fence and don't let the habit start in the first place, the better off you both will be.

If your dog comes to you with this habit or has developed it already, you may need professional help from a dog trainer. Try to lure him away and disrupt his focus on the fence and never leave him unattended in the backyard.

Leash aggression can only be dealt with through avoidance. When your dog sees another dog or person and becomes alert or excited, turn and walk in another direction. Your dog will feel safer and not become highly upset.

Do not try to confront his fears head-on by walking up to other dogs on a leash or tugging on the leash. He is reacting to fear and needs to feel safe, not further threatened.

Separation Anxiety

Some dogs become very worried when left alone. *Separation anxiety* means that the dog is feeling fear and worry just because he is alone. This is not the same as a bored dog or a dog that has too much energy. Bored or high-energy dogs may destroy things when left alone, but this is from having a lot of energy or boredom. A dog with separation anxiety is different. He becomes afraid and worried even when left for very short amounts of time. He might pee or poop in the house even

though he is well house-trained. He might even pee or poop right after you leave. This is not because he is bad or needed to "go." He may also destroy furniture, bark loudly, scratch on the door, run around from room to room, and cause other kinds of destruction in the house. If in a crate, he may shred his bedding and poop in the crate. He can't control his fear and he can't stop destroying things when he's alone.

This feels very odd to us, as we know there is nothing for him to be afraid of. Separation anxiety is easier to avoid than to cure. If you have a dog younger than a year old, make sure he has lots of good stimulating experiences and isn't left home alone.

It is during puppyhood that most dogs begin to feel separation anxiety. It is caused by poor socialization when he was a puppy.

If you have an older dog with this problem, it won't be easy to fix. Try this method:

- Before you need to leave the house, ignore your dog for twenty minutes.
- Do not give him a big good-bye or show him attention. Keep everything calm before you go.
- Practice picking up keys or putting on your shoes, things you do just before you go out. But then take your shoes off, set the keys down. Do this several times.
- Give him a good chew toy that you know he likes
- Leave the house and return. Don't greet your dog
- Get him used to you leaving and returning right away before he can start to howl or tear apart the couch.
- When you return, ignore him. Only pet him or greet him when he is calm.

Your dog may take time to learn not to be afraid when alone. While you are solving the habit, ignore any bad behavior or destruction that happened. Remember, he can't control this. He isn't bad, and punishing him will only make him more fearful and scared when you leave.

9 Healthy Dogs Are Happy Dogs

Kenney and Reggie

Kenney's favorite red sock was laying on her bed, wet with a hole chewed in it. Kenney was angry because she loved those socks and wore them all the time. She had just taken them off before her shower and meant to put them in the laundry. She looked around for Reggie, her eight-month-old Labrador/Pit Bull mixed-breed dog. Kenney found Reggie with the other red sock poking out of her mouth as she gripped it between her front paws. Kenney scolded her and ran to pull the sock free, but Reggie saw her coming and swallowed it. Now there was a much bigger problem than a chewed-up sock.

Kenney's mom called their veterinarian to ask what they should do. The vet asked them to bring Reggie in for an exam. Reggie was very happy and didn't seem at all upset by the sock she'd eaten. At the office, the vet explained that sometimes socks will pass through, but sometimes they don't. It might get stuck in the intestines and require surgery. She said that dogs love to chew on socks and underwear because they smell so much like the people they love. Since Reggie had just eaten the sock, it probably hadn't gone past her stomach. They could give her medicine to throw up. As soon as the medicine was injected, Reggie got sick and vomited. Out came the sock. Kenney was happy that Reggie would be okay and wouldn't need surgery.

Good Health Starts with Staying Lean

All dogs have the same basic needs to stay healthy. They need good food, clean water, a safe home, exercise, and regular veterinary visits. The way to good health for a dog is not much different than the way to good health for the rest of the family. Just like people, dogs need to eat good, nutritious food. Unlike people, most dogs are not very picky. That makes finding a food they will eat much easier than it is for a human child. It also means they will eat just about anything that looks or smells like it could be food, including socks.

BATH TIME

Baths should be fun and enjoyable for both you and your dog. Your dog will need a bath every now and then, so practice making it fun right from the start. Dogs love to roll in very stinky things and may even be sprayed by a skunk. Have everything you need ready for a dog bath and keep it together. If your dog comes in the house smelling particularly terrible, you will be able to take care of it quickly.

Things that are handy for a bath:

- Gentle dog shampoo and conditioner
- Rubber mitt or brush for scrubbing
- Large-toothed comb for long-haired dogs
- Soft towel
- Cotton balls for ears
- Plastic cup or bowl for dipping water
- Carrying caddy

Put cotton balls in her ears. Floppy-eared dogs can get an ear infection if water runs into the ear canal. Fill the tub with warm (not hot, not cold) water, but not past her ankle joints. Using a bowl or cup, pour warm water gently over your dog, starting at the neck and working your way back to the tail. Rub small amounts of shampoo into her fur and rinse using your bowl or cup. If you have a handheld sprayer, that is best for rinsing. Do the same with the conditioner. Make sure all the soap is rinsed out. This can take several rinses if her coat is thick.

When done, squeeze water out of the fur using your hands like a squeegee. Let her shake a few times and then towel her off with a soft, dry towel. Big dogs may need more than one towel. A hair dryer on low and cool can help speed the drying process.

Don't let her outside until she is dry. After a bath, don't be surprised if she runs around like a lunatic. Most dogs feel really good after a bath and want to bounce and play.

The commercial dog foods that you can buy in a store are an easy way to make sure your dog gets all the protein, vitamins, and minerals that he needs to be healthy. Follow the directions on the bag for how much to feed your dog. Dry kibble is healthy for your dog and makes feeding easy. The crunchy, dry kibble helps keep his teeth shiny and clean. Making your own food is possible, but it takes a lot more work to make sure your pup is getting all the nutrition he needs every day.

Don't overfeed your dog. Most dogs will eat whatever is put out, even if it is too much. Small dogs, like Beagles, need very little food but are masterful at convincing you they must have more.

Overfeeding causes a dog to gain weight and can cause other health problems. Obese dogs do not live as long, have more joint problems, and have a higher risk of cancer. It might be hard to ignore your dog's begging and drooling, but don't feed more than he needs. You have complete control over how much your dog eats and it is the easiest way to keep him healthy. A dog at a healthy weight may live one or two years longer than an overweight dog.

The chart on the next page will help you figure out if your dog is at a good, healthy weight.

Plenty of exercise and play will also help your dog build muscle and keep his weight down.

Dog Body Condition Chart

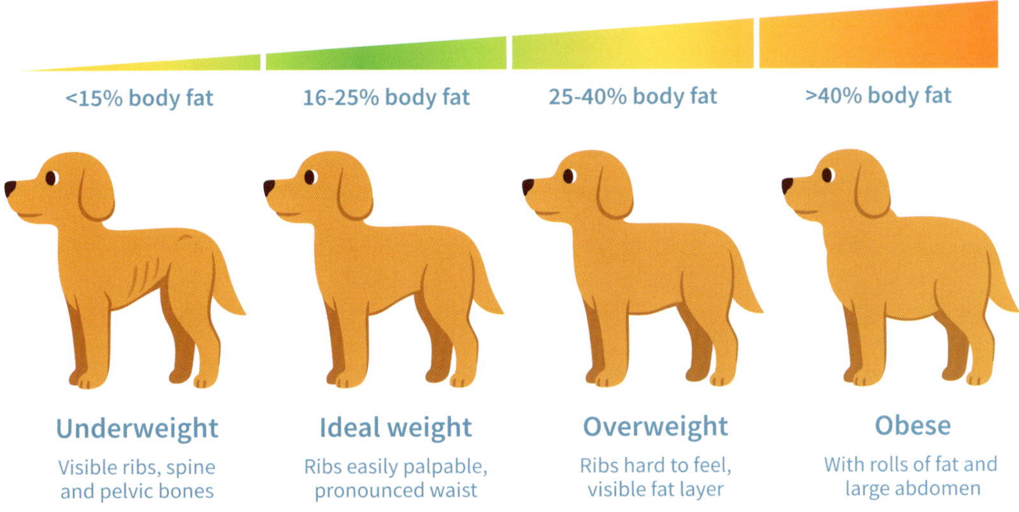

If you are using a lot of training treats, you may need to feed smaller meals. If your dog really loves her kibble, you can save out some of her breakfast to use for her training treats.

The only thing your dog should drink is water. Make sure her bowl stays clean and full of fresh water. Wash both her food and water bowls every day with warm soapy water. Some bowls can go in the dishwasher. Drooly dogs may need their bowls cleaned after every meal.

Visiting the Vet

Regular visits to your local veterinarian are an important part of keeping your dog healthy. Plan to go once a year if all is going well. Your veterinarian will do a well-dog checkup to make sure she has no problems and give her yearly vaccinations. Most

EAR GROOMING

Dog ears might flop over, perk straight up, or be a combination of perky and floppy. No matter the style of ear, keeping them clean and healthy is important. Look inside your dog's ears and smell them. If they look dirty or have a bad smell, you should clean them.

Use an ear cleaner recommended by your vet. An ear cleaner helps loosen the dirt and wax that build up. Drip a little into the ear and massage the ear with your fingers. This actually feels good and your dog may lean into your hand. Your dog will probably try to shake his head, and that's okay. Using a cotton ball or small piece of gauze, wipe out all of the cleaner from the outer ear. Don't poke deep into the ear canal, and never use a Q-tip or pointed object. That can do real damage. You may use several cotton balls to get all the cleaner, wax, and dirt out. Make sure to give your dog plenty of treats and praise.

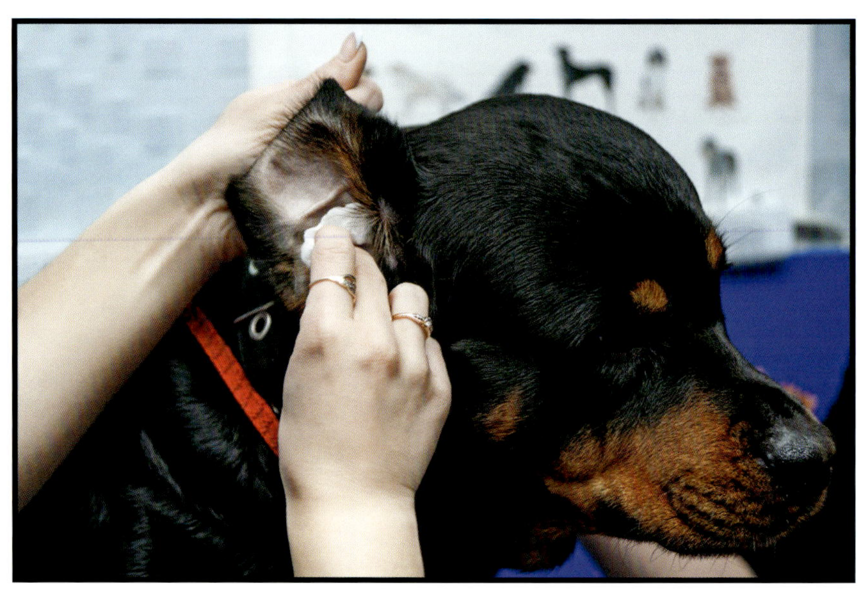

towns and counties require all dogs to be vaccinated against rabies. Your vet will also want to give vaccines or boosters for other diseases, and talk to you about flea and tick prevention.

At a regular vet checkup, your dog will be weighed, her eyes and ears checked, and her heart listened to, and the vet will examine her body looking for lumps, fleas and ticks, and sore spots.

Regular checkups help prevent serious problems from going unnoticed. Your vet will answer your questions and give you good advice. Your vet is probably a dog owner or lover—that's why they became a veterinarian! Your veterinarian does not want to hurt your dog, but some things they have to do may be uncomfortable for her.

RABIES

For centuries, rabies has been one of the most feared diseases. Rabies is always fatal. There is no cure and no treatment. The only way to survive rabies is to be vaccinated. Rabies is a disease of all mammals—it can kill people, dogs, cats, bats, raccoons, and all other warm-blooded creatures that have fur or hair. Rabies is spread through a bite by an infected animal. Almost every case of rabies in humans is due to a bite from a rabid dog. The rabies vaccine is very effective and can prevent you and your pet from dying a painful and terrifying death. Most local governments require proof of vaccination in dogs and will hold low-cost or free clinics to get the rabies vaccine. This is the best way of preventing your dog from getting rabies.

Most dogs dread visiting the vet. They know when you pull in the parking lot where you are and may not want to get out of the car or walk into the building. All of the training you do with your dog will help her deal with regular vet visits. Make sure she is okay with having her whole body touched. Every day, you should run your hands over her head, legs, back, tail, and stomach. If she is ticklish about any part of her, use treats and your normal training methods to teach her that she can let you touch any part of her. If you think your dog might bite the vet, tell them when you first arrive. She will have to wear a muzzle, which keeps the vet and her staff safe.

Your veterinarian's exam will make sure that everything is normal and healthy with your dog. She may ask you to bring a small amount of poop (called a "stool sample") to be checked for worms and parasites. She may also take some blood from your dog to check for heartworm. Dogs may get parasites from eating things off the ground. Your vet will be able to look through a microscope and tell you if there are any signs of worms.

For most dogs, a yearly trip to the vet for vaccinations and a checkup are all they will need. Emergency trips to the vet are possible, no matter how careful you are, so you should know what to expect. Before an emergency happens, be prepared. You should have the phone number for your regular veterinary office and an emergency twenty-four-hour veterinary clinic (for times when your regular vet's office is closed) saved in your house. The refrigerator is a good place to post it.

If your dog is showing signs of pain and distress, you should call the vet. Here are some examples of when you should call or take your dog in for an emergency.

- Bleeding or a deep wound
- Trouble breathing
- Falling down or stumbling
- If she's eaten something bad or toxic (*see* page 35)
- Sudden biting or scratching at herself, especially if she's scratching very hard or making herself bleed
- Vomiting frequently or with blood

If anything on this list happens, you should call your veterinarian immediately.

Dogs are known to eat things they shouldn't and may vomit once or twice. If your dog does this, but then seems okay, happy, and acting normal, watch her for a few hours. Vomiting a lot and looking tired and being uninterested in food could be a sign of something more serious. If your dog swallowed an object, it could be blocking her intestines. If she can't throw it up or poop it out, she will need a veterinarian to remove it surgically. Swallowing things is a problem, especially for young dogs. To avoid trips to the vet for emergency care, keep small objects that she might swallow out of reach.

PREVENTING PUPPIES

Female dogs are able to become pregnant and have puppies after they are about six months to one year of age. Male dogs mature at about the same rate. Unless you make an effort to prevent pregnancies, most dogs will have at least one litter of puppies every year. You may think this sounds great. Puppies are wonderful fun and you may even think that raising puppies could be an easy way to make money. Unfortunately, the reality is that there are far more puppies and dogs than there are homes for them. Every year, thousands of dogs and puppies must be killed (sometimes also called being euthanized) because there are too many of them and not enough homes. These are healthy dogs that could make wonderful pets. Thousands of homes cannot be found every year to save these dogs. Instead, it is important to prevent dogs from having puppies.

There is a safe procedure for dogs to prevent puppies. For female dogs it is called *spay* and male dogs it is called *neuter*. You might also hear this called “fixing” or “altering” the dog. Spaying or neutering is a simple surgery done by a veterinarian. It is done in a single day where your dog is dropped off in the morning and picked up that afternoon. Not only does it prevent unwanted puppies, but dogs that have been altered have longer and healthier lives. Male dogs are less aggressive and less likely to roam away from home. Spay and neuter surgeries will also prevent some cancers.

Pet dogs that have puppies are expensive to care for and a lot of work. With so many unwanted dogs dying every year, it is best to spay and neuter.

Grooming for Beginners

Dogs come with a variety of coat lengths, thicknesses, and shedding. Whatever your dog's coat type, it will need attention from time to time to keep the fur clean and reduce any unpleasant odors.

You will need different types of brushes or combs, depending on the length and thickness of her fur. Thick fur will need a slicker brush. In the spring, when your dog is shedding, a slicker brush will pull the dead, shedding hair out of his coat. If you don't brush out the dead hair, it will tangle and mat with live hair. Mats are dense tangles and knots in the fur. If left in the fur they can cause all kinds of problems. They will hold moisture and keep the skin underneath from properly drying. Mats can cause irritation and skin sores.

If your dog gets mats in his fur, remove them using a special comb with sharp edges or dog-safe scissors. A serrated comb like this works well.

HARDEST-TO-GROOM BREEDS

Long, silky fur and double-layered coats are the hardest to groom and keep clean and tangle-free. If you own one of these breeds (or crosses with these breeds) expect your life to include a lot of grooming.

- Afghan Hound
- Bichon Frise
- Chow Chow
- Bearded and Rough Coat Collies
- Maltese
- Puli
- Irish, English, and Gordon Setters

These breeds with thick fur and long, silky fur will get mats and tangles if not brushed twice a week or more. Collies and setters have fur that will tangle and mat easily. They also shed every spring. The Afghan has long silky fur that requires constant maintenance to keep it clean and tangle free.

The grooming is worth the effort. You will have a gorgeous dog with a beautiful soft coat if you groom every day.

As you brush out fur, feel your dog's skin for anything that shouldn't be there. Burrs, seeds, and other plant parts can get tangled in fur. Pull these out gently before they become deeply tangled. A bit of olive oil or cooking spray can be a good way of loosening burrs and pulling them out before they turn into a mat and have to be cut out.

Dogs with short hair require much less effort. You can run a soft brush or soft, bumpy mitt over their fur to stimulate the skin and keep them clean.

TOENAILS

Keeping your dog's toenails trimmed is important. Long toenails can make your dog walk funny, scratch your floors, and accidentally injure you or herself. Most dogs hate having their nails trimmed. Don't get into a fight with your dog over her nails. Before getting the nail clipper out, make sure she is used to you handling her feet and rubbing your fingers on and between her nails. Do this from early puppyhood through adult so it is just a normal part of petting.

When you start clipping, take off only a little at first. You might only be able to do one nail the first time. If she's very upset by nail trimming, you can work slowly to get her used to it. If she gives any sign that she might bite, stop and ask a groomer or the vet do the job. Walking her on pavement or hard ground is a good way to keep the nails short between trims.

This may be all the grooming a short-coated dog needs. No matter the coat length, feel under the ears and look in the fur for things like thorns, burrs, or ticks. The attention every day will make your dog happy and keep building a strong positive relationship.

RESCUE
DOG

10

Dogs with Jobs

Malik and Oliver

Malik noticed a dog with a harness on walking alongside a man in a wheelchair at the local convenience store. It was unusual to see a dog inside a store. Unlike his friends' dogs, this one was calm, not pulling on his leash, and standing quietly next to the wheelchair. Malik went over to the man in the wheelchair and asked if the dog was friendly and if he could pet him. The man thanked Malik for asking first but said that dog was working and couldn't play or be petted by strangers while on the job. The man was nice and told Malik that the dog's name was Oliver and that he was a trained service dog. Oliver helped him with his shopping and lots of other

things. Malik watched as the man directed Oliver to pick things off the shelves with his teeth and put them in a basket. It was amazing to watch Oliver. He was well-trained but was wagging his tail and happy. Oliver was happy doing work for the man in the wheelchair.

Dogs are unique in the animal world for the way they are able to perform so many different jobs. Dogs started working with humans to hunt and herd, guard, and protect. They continue to do these things, but less often. Hunting is now mostly a sport, not something humans need to do to survive.

FOSTERING A SERVICE DOG

Service dogs need to be adults when they begin their training. Before that, they need homes to live in. Most assistance-dog training organizations will breed their own puppies, especially if they are using a particular breed. Not all dogs are able to do the hard work of being a service dog. It helps to choose breeds and carefully raise them for a job. For the one to two years that a future service dog needs to grow up, foster families are needed.

While fostering a service puppy, a family will learn how to do basic obedience and socialization and get a puppy used to all the things that they will have to deal with in their job. A foster family may take their puppy to the beach on vacation, ride on an airplane, or go shopping. Foster families are very important. This is an excellent way for people who love dogs and want to help make the world a better place. You may have a service-dog training group near you. Fostering a puppy for a year or more is fun and rewarding, and you will learn a lot about training a puppy. It is difficult to give the puppy up after fostering, but the rewards of knowing how much good he will do in someone's life that really needs him makes it worth the effort.

The instincts and abilities of dogs are now being put to other uses. As dogs find new jobs and new ways to work with humans, we are amazed at our dogs' capacity to learn and do a stunning variety of jobs.

The number one job for most pet dogs now is to be a loyal and loving companion. Even as companions, dogs continue to find lots of ways of being useful. They motivate us to exercise, they clean up spilled food, and they bring joy. The job of companion dog is just fine for many dogs. They are happy to live in our homes and do little of the work they were originally bred to do. For more exuberant dogs, there are new sports, games, and activities. Some of these are becoming competitive and many are just for fun.

While that is important, there are a vast number of other jobs that dogs work everyday. Dogs save lives, risk danger, and help people with special needs, just to name a few of the important jobs dogs do.

Dogs have fantastic smelling and sniffing abilities. Their noses are thousands of times more sensitive than ours. They can tell the difference between the smells of individual people so well that a trained dog can track and find a missing child from a single article of clothing. Dogs can find plants in luggage, a human buried in a collapsed building, or drugs hidden in a car. When trained to sniff out a particular scent, they can reliably find that scent despite many other smells mixed in. Dogs' noses are so reliable, judges will allow them to be used in court. Many dog jobs involve using their noses.

DOGS AT AIRPORTS

In 1984, the "Beagle Brigade" was created at a Los Angeles airport to help find plants and animal products that should not be brought into the country. Beagles were chosen because they have excellent sniffing abilities, are small and nonthreatening to passengers, and are highly motivated by food to sniff out things. You may see beagles, and now other dog breeds, at many airports where international flights arrive in the country. Dogs can distinguish easily between the many things a traveler may bring with them and pick out just those items that are not allowed. Sandwiches, lotion, toothpaste—these all have strong smells that a beagle must learn to ignore. Plants may carry pests or diseases that can spread rapidly if brought into the country. A plant may have no strong scent to a person, but a beagle can pick it out even if there

are other, stronger-smelling items in the suitcase with the plant. The beagles you see are protecting our food sources and keeping our agriculture safe.

Dogs have many other jobs in airports. Therapy dogs are common. They provide comfort to travelers who may be worried or anxious about flying. Therapy dogs at airports wear a special vest to identify them as a dog that it is okay to pet or hug. Specially trained dogs, usually Border Collies, are used at a small number of airports to chase wildlife off runways. As a natural predator, a dog does not harm the environment or the wildlife but will keep airplanes and passengers safe.

Finally, some dogs with a great deal of specialized training are in airports to detect things that may be dangerous, such as bombs, ammunition, or other weapons. Dogs also can detect most illegal drugs and money. The US government has two large detection dog training centers in Virginia and Texas. Today, over 1,500 dogs have jobs in the US Department of Homeland Security detecting everything from flowers to firearms.

DOGS IN MOVIES

We fall in love with movie dogs every year. Dogs on TV and in movies become instant celebrities. After a successful movie is released with a dog hero, demand for puppies of the same breed often increases as new dog owners want to have a puppy just like the one they fell in love with in the movie. The very first movie star dog was in a black-and-white movie with no sound that was produced in 1905. The star of the movie was a collie named Blair. The entire movie was just six minutes long (and you can watch it today on YouTube).

The name of the movie was *Rescued by Rover*. The plot was simple. A baby is kidnapped and the family dog, Rover, finds the child and helps return her to her family. During those six minutes, Rover opens doors, swims across a river, runs through city traffic, and convinces the baby's father to follow him to find the baby. The movie was an instant success. The name Rover, which had been rare for dogs, became the top dog name of the time (and continues to be a popular name for dogs even now).

Some of the most famous movie and television dogs are:

- **Lassie**, a Collie, began in 1947 as a radio program, then transferred into the movies in 1954 with twelve movies created over sixty years (with different dogs playing the lead role), six television series (two animated), and many "cameo" appearances in other programs and game shows. Lassie also appeared in over fifty fiction books for all ages of readers.

- **Toto**, a Cairn Terrier appeared in *The Wizard of Oz* in 1939. Toto was played by a single, female dog named Terry. Terry had roles in sixteen other movies, but only *The Wizard of Oz* became a huge hit. Terry was one of the highest-paid actors in the movie, earning $125 per day, which was more than the Munchkin character actors were paid and more than most working Americans earned in a day.
- **Beethoven**, a 190-pound (86-kg) Saint Bernard who starred in eight movies beginning in 1992; the wildly successful movie led to an animated television series and children's books. The role of Beethoven was played by several different Saint Bernard dogs, as the original dog died after the second movie at the age of twelve, which is quite old for a Saint Bernard dog.
- **Scooby-Doo**, an animated Great Dane who started as a lovable dog that solved mysteries in an animated television series in 1969 has been turned into live-action movies, books, and animated movies.
- **Perdy and Pongo**, an animated pair of Dalmatians with fifteen puppies, featured in *101 Dalmatians*—and then there were ninety-nine puppies after the big rescue. The movie was a huge hit in 1961 when it was first released and led to a remake using live dogs in 1996. It took 230 puppies and twenty adult dogs to film all the scenes to make the movie in 1996.

Dogs hear far better than people. They can pick up sounds far too soft for us to hear and they also hear frequencies much higher than human ears can hear. Their excellent hearing makes it easy for them to hear approaching danger or the family car coming down the street. Some dogs seem to be able to predict earthquakes due to their very sensitive hearing. They are particularly good at hearing very high pitches that human ears can't hear.

Dogs are faster and more agile than humans. Teaching them to go away from their handler and run at top speed makes them excellent at jobs in police work.

Due to their phenomenal noses, ears, speed, and agility, dogs are able to do many jobs that humans, and other animals, can't. Dogs have always been useful to people, but the ways in which they continue to do work, and find new jobs, is like no other animal. The list of jobs that dogs can do well, or better than any other animal, is long and impressive.

Search and Rescue

Dogs are specially trained to be search-and-rescue dogs. Any breed, or mixed breed, can take on this job. The work is hard, and the hours of training are very long. The most important quality is that the dog has a strong desire to find. Dogs that are bred to hunt will have strong instinct to find things, especially using their noses. Search-and-rescue dogs likely come from some of the hunting dog or working dog breeds. This instinct to hunt is called "prey drive." For search-and-rescue dogs, wanting to please their handler isn't enough, they need to love the job of "finding."

A NOSE WITH A DOG ATTACHED

Bloodhounds have the most amazing and exceptional nose in the dog world. Bloodhounds are called "a nose with a dog attached" because they seem to have magical abilities to use their noses in ways we can't really imagine. A Bloodhound's nose starts by having far more olfactory cells or "scent receptors." Their long ears and large lips may also help catch and bring in scent, funneling it into the nose.

Standing in a big field, a Bloodhound might get a whiff of wind in his nose, giving him a detailed picture of everything that has a chemical signature in scent (which is just about everything). He will "see" the thousands of things that live and move in that field. If a person walked through days before, the Bloodhound can pick up the scent and follow it alone, ignoring other scents and distractions.

The entire biology of a Bloodhound is designed to create the world's most perfect scent tracking creature. Part of the reason for a Bloodhound's success is his willingness to stay on a track for hours no matter the weather or roughness of the ground. No human invention or technological advance has come close to doing what a Bloodhound can do. Bloodhounds have such a strong desire to track, they can sometimes be miserable pets and unhappy living a quiet life. Bloodhounds thrive when put on a scent and are happiest when they have a job to do.

Search-and-rescue dogs are usually medium to large, fit, and able to work for long hours. The Federal Emergency Management Agency (FEMA) has over 250 teams of trained search-and-rescue dogs that are located across the United States. Dogs train at twenty-eight locations in as many different environments and confronting as many different obstacles as possible. Dogs need to be confident and able to work no matter the weather or situation.

Search-and-rescue dogs are called in when people may be trapped under a collapsed building after a disaster, such as a tornado, hurricane, or earthquake. Dogs in search and rescue must be adults and mature enough to handle the work. Dogs must be at least eighteen months old, but most are over two years of age. Every three years the dogs have to be retested to make sure they can still do the job. The most common types of dog in the FEMA search-and-rescue teams are Labrador, German Shepherd, Golden Retriever, Malinois, and Border Collie. These dogs need to be fit, smart, and agile and have a good nose.

If a person is buried under several feet of rubble, a search-and-rescue dog will be able to smell them and maybe hear them if they can speak. Dogs are able to crawl across unsteady materials easily. They are much better at safely moving around the disaster area to find people in trouble without getting hurt.

Handlers of search-and-rescue dogs have a very close bond with their dog. A dog needs to trust her handler, and the handler has to trust the dog. Handlers and dogs train together all the time and in many different places. Dogs do not switch handlers. The dog-handler relationship can take years to build. Once a dog and handler have worked and trained together, they can read each other's signals in a way that looks invisible to a person watching. The dog's reactions as they are searching and locating people are specific to that dog, and the handler must know what each of the dog's reactions mean. Most important, a search-and-rescue dog needs to love to work. Finding people in rubble and saving their lives needs to be fun for the dog. Good handlers train with lots of praise and squeaky toys to keep the job fun.

Service and Assistance Dogs

Dogs improve the lives of families everywhere, but some dogs are specially trained to help people with particular issues. These dogs are called *service dogs* or *assistance dogs*.

We have a long history of using dogs for assistance. In the year 1780 in France, dogs were trained to help blind people. Only a small number of dogs were trained, but the idea caught on. By the time of World War I, there was a big need for guide dogs. Many soldiers returned from the war blind and unable to see, drive, or safely move about. These were young men, and they didn't want to give up their freedom in life. Several special schools started to train guide dogs for blind veterans. Over time, better training was developed, and dogs were trained around the world to help blind people of all ages, not just veterans. Foundations now provide guide dogs to blind people free of charge. It is very expensive to train these guide dogs to be the eyes for someone that cannot see. Guide dogs must be able to make decisions, walk through busy public spaces and city streets, and keep their person safe from obstacles such as tree branches or construction. These amazing dogs are able to help people live full and independent lives.

Specially trained service dogs help people with many different kinds of disabilities. A service dog can be trained to be the "ears" for the Deaf and hearing-impaired. Hearing dogs will let their owners know when there are common, but important, sounds. This could be a doorbell, an oven timer, or a crying baby. A hearing dog will nudge or paw her person and lead him to where the sound is coming from. A hearing dog can alert her owner to a fast-approaching bicycle or car that could put him in danger. Most hearing dogs are small-to-medium mixed-breed dogs. They need to be intelligent, friendly, and willing to pay attention to sounds. They also can't react to unimportant background noises. It is difficult to teach a dog how to figure out what is important and what is not.

Service dogs can be trained to help people who use wheelchairs. They can pick up dropped items, open doors, and flip light switches on or off. They are able to go well beyond the basic assistance training once they are paired with a person. A bond is formed, and the partnership grows. An assistance dog can seem to know what his person needs and help, even if it's something he was never trained to do.

11

Fun Things to Do with Dogs

Reina and Cheyenne

Reina knew her dog Cheyenne was bored. Cheyenne was a three-year-old Shetland Sheepdog. Shetland Sheepdogs, also called "Shelties," are super smart, small herding dogs. Reina didn't have sheep; she lived in a suburb where sheep aren't allowed. Reina's mom told her to walk Cheyenne more and to take her to the dog park for exercise, but it was never enough. Cheyenne had too much energy and Reina was bored with taking long walks that never seemed to tire her out.

Reina did some research on the internet

and found a dog group near her that did agility training, which sounded like fun. Reina and her mom drove to watch a practice and talk to the people doing agility with their dogs. It looked like something Cheyenne would enjoy. She was a very friendly dog, but her energy was too much for most other dogs at the dog park. Agility might be just the thing. Reina brought Cheyenne to practice. They learned some basic skills. At first, it was slow, and Reina had to do a lot of running, but Cheyenne eventually figured it out. She was best at jumping over or through things. Reina and Cheyenne went to more practices and tried new obstacles. Reina had a lot of fun, too. She had to run along and learn the commands. This was much better than walking up and down the street. Cheyenne was a natural. Even though they made mistakes, they both got better and faster.

Dog Sports

Dogs are naturally active and athletic. They are fast, strong, and smart. Your dog could be an excellent athlete. Maybe someday there will be a Dog Olympics! Until then, you and your dog can train for a bunch of competitive dog sports, or you can find lots of ways to have fun with your dog that don't involve winning or losing. New dog sports are created every year. Whether you want to compete or not, there are many ways to strengthen your relationship with your furry friend by getting active and involved in an activity.

Dogs have a lot of athletic abilities—most dogs are able to run fast, jump over things, and turn quickly. They aren't great climbers but can manage slopes and things on an angle. Most dogs can handle the demands of a sport. If your dog is over ten years old or has any kind of health problem, check with your vet before signing your dog up for a sport. Young puppies should not do demanding sports until they are at least six months old. Different sports have different rules on how old your puppy should be before starting to train. If your dog is healthy and between one and ten years old, go for it! Your dog (and you!) will love the fun things you can do together. You will be amazed at the things dogs can learn to do and get really good at.

Agility

Dog agility combines speed, flexibility, and jumping in a fast-paced, exciting sport. Agility dogs leap over jumps, thread through a maze of poles, climb ladders and slides, and shoot through tunnels at top speed. A good agility dog needs to be quick, smart, and brave and he has to trust his handler.

To get started in agility, your dog needs to have basic obedience training. He also must have lots of energy and a desire to run, and he should get along well with other dogs. Start by

THE IDITAROD

There is a famous sled dog race that takes place every year in Alaska. The race is almost 1,000 miles (1,610 km) long and takes between seven and twenty days to complete. It crosses two mountain ranges. Bad weather is always possible. Sled dog teams start this grueling race with strict rules to protect the life and health of the sled dogs, including about fifty veterinarians along the racecourse. The dogs used in this race are usually Siberian Huskies, because their thick fur, strength, and desire to run and pull make them ideal. The person on the sled directing the dogs is called a "musher."

The Iditarod Trail Sled Dog Race is based on a true story from 1925. Children in Nome, Alaska, were dying from a terrible disease called diphtheria. Nome is a tiny town at the eastern edge of Alaska. Nome is remote and not near either of Alaska's large cities, Anchorage and Juneau. It was almost impossible to get to Nome during the winter. The only cure to save the children was a special medicine, or serum. The serum was in Anchorage, which was almost 700 miles away. The weather was terrible, and planes could not deliver the serum. The serum was taken by railroad as close as possible, but it was still a long, difficult journey where there were no roads or vehicles that could get through in January. Only teams of sled dogs, working together in a relay, could save the lives of the children. The sled dogs made the trip with the serum despite harsh weather. There were twenty teams of drivers and dogs that

ran the serum to Nome. The longest leg was run by a lead dog named Togo. The final leg of the trip was completed by the lead dog Balto, who arrived in Nome on February 2, 1925.

The Iditarod race has been running for over fifty years to celebrate the bravery and history of Alaskan dogs and people.

Kids over the age of fourteen can compete in a shorter 160-mile (257-km) sled dog race that takes two days. The young mushers must pack enough food for themselves and all their dogs, camp outside, deal with extreme cold and wind, and care for their dogs overnight by themselves in the Junior Iditarod, just as the adults do in the longer Iditarod race. Winners of the Junior Iditarod can win a dog sled, a fur hat, musher mittens, and a scholarship worth thousands of dollars. It is a difficult, demanding race that requires young mushers to train and prepare for years.

finding a local agility club or agility class near you. Once you've got the basics, you can practice at home with simple equipment that you can make yourself. At an agility competition, there will be a course of objects that each dog has to do in the same order. The winner is the fastest to complete the course without any errors. Your dog can't read the map, so he will rely on you to give fast, accurate instructions on where to go next. The partnership between an agility dog and his handler is so strong, the dog will follow the handler's signals and barely slow down between obstacles. Agility competitions are open to both purebred and mixed-breed dogs. Even if you never compete, practicing agility is great exercise for both you and your dog. And it's a lot of fun!

Hunting Sports and Field Trials

The American Kennel Club has many different options for dogs who were originally bred to hunt. The Sporting Group dogs will hunt birds. The Hound Group dogs will hunt mammals. For both of these groups, there are competitions to test how well dogs perform the hunting skills they were bred to do. Hunting instincts are deep and strong in these types of dogs. With some training and practice, you can see how well your dog does in these sports that tap into their ability to follow a trail, flush a bird, or run through tunnels after rodents. These dog breeds were some of the first to be developed by humans, and they are excellent at working side by side with hunters of all kinds. Hunting dogs have tremendous energy and can work all day in fields, water, woods, or tunnels.

DOCK DIVING

Does your dog love to swim? Consider teaching him the best sport for a hot summer day—dock diving! You throw your pup's favorite squeaky toy into a pool. Your dog waits on the dock until you tell him to go get the toy. He runs as fast as he can down the dock and leaps across the pool as far as possible. The dog that jumps the farthest wins! It's simple, and many dogs truly love this sport. There are dock diving contests for dogs all over. Labs, spaniels, and other breeds that love to swim are really good at dock diving. Mixed breeds can also compete. This is a fun activity to watch even if your dog doesn't particularly like swimming.

Even if you don't hunt, consider training your sporting or hound group dog to compete in a performance dog trial. There are almost fifteen different kinds of field-and-sport competitions. These are all a bit different depending on the kind of hunting dog. The field trials are competitions to see which dog is best at doing the types of things expected for that breed of performance dog. For example, Spaniel trials ask dogs to flush and retrieve on both land and water. Beagles and Basset Hounds may compete in a pack (small or large) to test their ability to hunt in a group and accurately follow a trail laid out with the scent of a rabbit.

Another fun sport is "coursing" or running after an object (or a lure) that is being pulled through a field at high speed and many changes of direction. Coursing is ideal for the big, fast sight hounds like the Borzoi or Afghan Hound. CAT (coursing ability test) and Fast CAT are variations on coursing that are open to all dogs. They chase a lure and are judged on speed and their willingness to stay focused on the lure.

Dachshunds and small Terriers can become Earthdog competitors. They need to find a hole with the scent of a rodent in it. They are judged on their ability and willingness to hunt underground. There are many other sports that you can find for your dog. Some are for a particular breed group, but many are now open to all dogs and mixed breeds.

You can find groups training for many of these sports in your local area. Dog lovers are always willing to help new dogs learn their sport. You might find a local fun day or training group to get started and see if your dog wants to be an athlete.

Dog Shows

Dog shows are competitions to see which dog is closest to "perfect" according to the breed standard. A judge will look at conformation, or how well the dog's bones and muscles are put together. In a traditional dog show, conformation is the most important part of judging. Each breed is judged separately, and each has its own standard. Beautiful, clean fur is the easiest part to see, as many show dogs have long, beautiful, perfectly groomed fur. All aspects of the dog are judged to find the best, healthiest, and most correct dog of the breed.

For example, a bulldog should have a short, flat nose. Most winning bulldogs will have an underbite (the bottom teeth will stick out further than the top teeth).

For most other breeds, an underbite is a flaw that might disqualify the dog from even showing. Dog show people have to know all the details for their breed standard if they want to do well in the show ring. At a purebred dog show, dog owners need to have registration papers to enter and compete. If you have a purebred dog, a breed show can be fun and an interesting way to learn about your dog's breed.

Most dog shows are run by the rules of the American Kennel Club. The most famous dog

4-H

If you love to "do" and "learn by doing" then you will love 4-H. Over six million kids and teenagers across the country belong to local 4-H clubs to work on projects that interest them. Many 4-H clubs have a "dog project" where kids can learn from professional dog trainers and handlers (and many other animal and nonanimal projects, too!). 4-H was created over one hundred years ago through the US Department of Agriculture. Now it's mainly run through local community extensions and public universities. It's a great place for you to learn about your dog and meet other kids that love and own dogs. You can compete through 4-H at your local country or state fair, or train and learn without competing. There is a lot to do and learn about dogs. 4-H can help you keep learning in a fun way.

show is held in New York City by the Westminster Kennel Club. The show is the oldest dog show in the United States and has run for over 140 years. While few dogs ever get to the Westminster dog show, there are lots of shows all over the country for dogs to strut their stuff and show off a little.

Other Cool Things to Do with Your Dog

You don't have to go to a dog show or compete in a sport to have a lot of fun with your dog. A great way to start is with the simple game of fetch. Throwing a ball or stick and asking your dog to bring it back and give it to you is the first step. Fetch can be taught to most dogs. Once your dog is chasing and bringing back a ball or stick, there's a lot more that you can do, but the basic commands are the same. Dogs love to play. Go ahead and teach your dog games you both can enjoy and keep building that strong relationship.

How to teach "fetch":

- Get a lot of bite-size treats your dog loves.
- Sit on the floor with the ball (or toy) that you will use to teach fetch. It's good to make this a "special" ball (or toy) that you only let her have when you are playing fetch together.
- Let her take the toy and praise her for holding it in her mouth

- Give her a treat when she lets go and praise again.
- Say the word "hold" when the ball is in her mouth and "give" when she lets go. Keep praising and giving treats.
- You want her to hold the ball until you ask her to give it. But this is going to be very short (just a few seconds at first).
- Set the ball a little bit away—not far! Don't throw it! She should be interested in chasing it. As soon as she picks it up, praise her and say "hold."
- Keep moving the toy a bit farther away. You can start using the words "fetch" or "get it."
- Praise and treat her when she gives it to you.
- Take it slow. Don't rush it.
- Stop before she's tired or bored and start again later or the next day

Once your dog understands that she should get and bring back the ball or toy, you can start throwing the ball gently. Only when she's always looking for it and willing to chase should you throw it farther.

You can build on this game by using the same words with other toys, like a Frisbee, or throwing a floating ball into water for her to fetch. There are lots of fun ways to play fetch once she's learned to chase, hold, and give you objects.

HOMEMADE TREATS

You can make fun and easy treats for your dog. Try mixing yogurt with chopped-up apples, blueberries, or carrots. Put the mixture in ice cube trays and freeze. Your dog will love these frozen yogurt and fruit treats.

You can make baked treats as well. Try this recipe with the help of a parent or adult.

Honey Dog Cookies

- 1 cup flour
- 1 cup oats
- 2 teaspoons baking powder
- 2 tablespoons butter
- 2 tablespoons honey
- 1 egg
- ½ cup milk

Mix all the ingredients together in a bowl. Using a rolling pin, roll the dough out flat and about ¼ inch thick. Using your favorite cookie cutter (dog bone-shaped cookie cutters are very cool!) cut out the cookies. Bake for 15–20 minutes in an oven set at about 375 to 400 degrees Fahrenheit (190 to 205 Celsius). Turn off the oven and let them slowly dry and cool for another two hours.

Try different ingredients to see what your dog loves best.

INDEX

ABOUT THE AUTHOR

Lynn Guelzow begged her way into her first job at the age of nine at her neighbor's boarding, grooming, and training kennel. This began a lifelong love of and fascination with dogs of all kinds. She trained dogs in obedience through 4-H as a kid and continued as an adult. Lynn has worked with dogs her entire life, from a small Jack Russell Terrier to a Great Dane mix. Her household has welcomed purebreds and mixed breeds. She's worked with rescue groups and fostered dogs and puppies. Lynn's home in Connecticut is a menagerie consisting of two dogs, a cat, and two horses—all of whom have learned to become happy family members through positive, consistent training.

NOTES